Helion & Company Limited
Unit 8 Amherst Business Centre
Budbrooke Road
Warwick
CV34 5WE
England
Tel. 01926 499 619
Fax 0121 711 4075
Email: info@helion.co.uk
Website: www.helion.co.uk
Twitter: @helionbooks
Visit our blog http://blog.helion.co.uk/

Published by Helion & Company 2019
Designed and typeset by Farr out
    Publications, Wokingham, Berkshire
Cover designed by Paul Hewitt, Battlefield
    Design (www.battlefield-design.co.uk)
Printed by Henry Ling Limited, Dorchester,
    Dorset

Text © Amaru Tincopa Gallegos 2019
Illustrations © as individually credited
Color profiles drawn by Luca Canossa ©
    Helion & Company Limited 2019
Maps drawn by Tom Cooper © Helion &
    Company Limited 2019

ISBN 978-1-911628-67-5

British Library Cataloguing-in-Publication
    Data
A catalogue record for this book is available
    from the British Library

We always welcome receiving book
proposals from prospective authors.

CONTENTS

ABBREVIATIONS

AAA	anti-aircraft artillery		EIEA	Strategic Reconnaissance and Attack Squadron (Peru)
AB	air base			
AME	*Aviación Militar Ecuatoriana* (Ecuadorean Military Aviation)		EIM	Reconnaissance Squadron of Naval Aviation (Peru)
BAE	Ecuadorean Navy Vessel		EOB	*Escuadrón de Observación y Bombardeo* (Observation & Bomber Squadron)
BAP	Peruvian Navy Vessel			
CAN	Naval Air Corps (Peru)		EP	Army of Peru
CGA	*Comandancia General de Aeronáutica* (Peruvian General Air Command)		GA	Air Group
			MGA	Navy (Peru)
CO	commanding officer		MMA	Navy and Aviation Ministry (Peru)
DL	Light Division (Peru)		SAE	Army Air Service (Peru)
EA	Aviation Squadron		TON	Northern Operational Theatre (Peru)
EB	Bombardment Squadron		TONO	North-Eastern Operational Theatre (Peru)
EC	Fighter Squadron			

1

ORIGINS

During most of the last 200 years, Ecuador and Peru have fought a series of wars over essentially the same issue: the question of the mutual border between the Andes mountain range and the Maranon River (a main tributary of the Amazon), including a part of the Amazonian basin. The conflict erupted almost as soon as Spain's colonial territories in South America declared their independence in 1810, and resulted in what was the longest-running international armed conflict in the Western Hemisphere. Air power began to play a role in the 1930s when, following the so-called Leticia Indecent, Peru found itself in possession of strong armed forces that had nothing to do.

Land of Hidden Treasures

The territory of modern-day Peru can be divided into three main topographical regions: the coastal plain, the sierra and the *montaña*. The coastal plain is an elongated stretch of land extending the entire length of the country, to the Atacama Desert of northern Chile, with few ports and oases in between. The desert plain is so dry that only 10 of the 52 rivers descending the Andean slopes to the Pacific Ocean have sufficient volume to maintain their flow across the desert to the ocean. The sierra, which covers some 30 per cent of the country's territory, is dominated by the towering mountain ranges of the Andes (including some of the highest peaks in the world), lofty plateaus, deep gorges and valleys, with an average elevation of 3,660m (about 12,000ft). In the north-east, the sierra slopes downward to a vast, flat tropical jungle, the *selvas*, extending to the Brazilian border and forming part of the Amazon Basin. The forested slopes and a less elevated region are collectively designated the *montaña*: covered with thick tropical forests in the west and with dense tropical vegetation in the centre and the east, this area constitutes about 60 per cent of the Peruvian land area: isolated from the rest of the country, this region remains largely unexplored and underdeveloped to this today.

The climate of Peru is as diverse as its topography, ranging from tropical in the *montaña* to arctic in the Andes, but the temperature in the coastal plain is normally equable, averaging about 20°C

throughout the year. This is further moderated by winds blowing from the cool offshore current known as the Peru, or Humboldt, Current. Nevertheless, the coast receives relatively little rain, largely because the area is dominated by the eastern trade winds. The *montaña* region is extremely hot and humid: the prevailing easterly winds blowing across that region gather moisture that is later deposited in the *cordilleras*. Peru's climate periodically experiences a weather pattern known as *El Niño*: this occurs every three to seven years when unusually warm ocean conditions appear along the western coast. During *El Niño*, the wet weather moves from the western Pacific to the east, bringing heavy rains that frequently cause extensive flooding.

Children of the Sun

The earliest traces of human presence on the territory nowadays within the borders of Peru have been dated to approximately 9,000 BC, when Andean societies based on agriculture – and already using irrigation and terracing – emerged. The oldest known complex society was the Norte Chico civilisation, which flourished along the coast of the Pacific Ocean between 3,000 and 1,000 BC. This was followed by a series of localised and specialised cultures that rose and fell – like the Chavin culture, from 1500–300 BC, and the Cupisnique culture that flourished from around 1000–200 BC, followed by the Paracas, Nazca, Wari and the more outstanding Chimo and Mochica – both on the coast and in the highlands. The outstanding among them were the Mochica, renowned for their irrigation system, and the Chimu, who were great city builders and lived in a loose confederation scattered along the northern coast and into what is nowadays southern Ecuador. Further inland, the Tiahuanaco culture developed near Lake Titicaca, while the Wari culture developed large urban settlements and wide-ranging state systems between AD 500 and 1000.

In the 15th Century, the Incas – originally one of the small and relatively minor ethnic groups – began to expand and incorporate their neighbours: over the following 100 years they formed by far the largest empire in pre-Columbian America. Under the rule of Emperor Pachacuti (considered to be the 'child of the sun') and his son, Topa

Francisco Pizarro's attack on Atahualpa in Cajamarca, on 16 November 1532. (Oil by Juan Lepiani)

Inca Yupanqui, they controlled a population of up to 16 million inhabitants, mostly in the Andean region, and a state ruled with the help of a comprehensive code of laws. Using a variety of methods – from conquest to peaceful assimilation – between 1438 and 1533 the Incas brought under their control all of western South America between the Patía River, nowadays in southern Colombia, and the Maule River in what is today Chile.

The Spanish Conquest

The Spanish made their first contact with the Inca Empire in 1526, when soldiers and *conquistadors* under Francisco Pizarro and Diego de Almagro began reconnoitring the northernmost Inca strongholds along the coast. In 1528, the Inca Emperor Huayna Capaca died from Spanish-introduced smallpox: the empire was subsequently devastated – and decimated – by this disease and by a civil war between his sons, Atahualpa and Huáscar. While Huáscar proclaimed himself Sapa Inca ('Only Emperor') in Cuzco, the army declared loyalty to Atahualpa, who was closer to, and had better relations with, its leading generals.

After being granted the licence to conquer the land the Spanish called 'Peru' (a word that may be an Indo-Hispanic hybrid) from the Queen of Spain in 1529, Pizarro launched his first expedition, leading 168 men on foot and 62 on horses, three years later. After four long expeditions he established the first Spanish settlement in northern Peru, calling it San Miguel de Piura. Preoccupied with fighting the war against Huáscar, Atahualpa was slow in reacting to the Spanish appearance. Furthermore, many of his followers considered the Spanish to be 'gods': they were tall, had their bodies fully wrapped in clothing, were armed with swords and firearms, and riding horses – animals unknown in Southern America. Although concluding that Pizarro and his troops were no gods after all, Atahualpa and his lieutenants decided to negotiate. However, Spanish insistence that the Inca emperor convert to Christianity, and communication problems then resulted in the Battle of Cajamarca, fought on 16 November 1532, in the course of which the Spaniards unleashed volleys of gunfire and cavalry charges at the mass of about 6,000 unarmed and shocked Incas, massacring up to 2,000 of them. Although greatly outnumbered, the Spanish captured Atahualpa, and during his captivity, they forced him to order his generals to back down by threatening to kill him if he did not. In return, Atahualpa offered to fill a large room with gold and promised the Spanish twice that amount in silver. Eager to obtain such a treasure, Pizarro had no intention of releasing the Inca chief. Instead, he held him in order to influence Atahualpa's generals and the population to maintain peace – while waiting for reinforcements. In February 1533, Almagro had joined him in Cajamarca with an additional 150 men and 50 horses. Although the treasure was delivered from Cuzco and continued flowing steadily from then on, and Atahualpa eventually converted to Christianity, he was garrotted on 29 August 1533.

In November of that year, Pizarro dispatched an expedition of 140 foot soldiers led by Benalcázar, one of his lieutenants, to conquer Quito. Benalcázar defeated the forces of the great Inca warrior Rumiñawi in a battle near the modern city of Riobamba (in Ecuador) and – reinforced by 500 gold-greedy men led by Guatemalan Governor Pedro de Alvarado – continued his advance. However, by the time he reached the abandoned fortress, it was empty of its treasures. Meanwhile, facing growing dissent, Pizarro installed successive puppet Inca rulers. However, this was to no avail, as Atahualpa's death meant there were no hostage left to deter the generals of the Incan army or prevent a popular uprising. By February 1536, the Spanish in Cuzco were under siege and four relief columns were wiped out.

This Inca success proved only temporary as the combination of superior Spanish weapons and internal disagreements collapsed Inca morale, and the army withdrew, never to return. Manco Inca did manage to establish a small state in the mountainous region of Vilacabamba, where he and his successors held power for few decades longer.

Despite the demise of the Inca Empire, the creation of the *Audiencia Real* (Royal Court) and the foundation of the City of Lima in 1535, Peru subsequently experienced outright catastrophe. A struggle for power between Pizarro and de Almagro resulted in a long civil war, which continued even after the latter was killed. Indeed, Almagro's descendants avenged his death by killing Pizarro in 1541. In 1572, Viceroy Francisco de Toledo arrived to destroy the Neo-Inca state: the last Inca ruler, Túpac Amaru, was murdered by the Spanish the same year and the Viceroyalty of Peru was established. The Inca civilisation – including all of its treasures and the unique indigenous road and communication systems – was subsequently completely destroyed, as all that mattered to the Spanish was gold. Worse still, infectious diseases wiped out up to 50 per cent of the native population, large parts of which were enslaved as servants and concubines, while those native groups that sided with the Spaniards were forcefully converted to Christianity. In the longer term, the conquest of Peru had massive repercussions for Spain too: as gold and silver mining became the primary source of income in the Viceroyalty, both countries flourished, fuelling a complex trade network that extended from the Philippines to Europe and included the Spanish import of African slaves. However, while the looted treasures from the former Inca Empire – along with the re-export of such crops as corn and potatoes – made Spain immensely rich and the superpower of the 16th and 17th centuries, the flood of gold and silver also caused inflation, converting the country into one of poorest nations of Europe by the 19th century.

Other direct results of the Spanish conquest included deep divisions within Peruvian society that last to this day, for at the top of the emerging country's social structure there has always been a minority of Spanish-speaking Europeans living on the coast, mainly in the Lima area. While only about 15 per cent of the population are of European descent, they controlled most of the wealth and political power until the late 20th Century. At the bottom are Quechua- and Aymara-speaking Native Americans living in the highlands and also in the shantytowns around Arequipa, Lima and other coastal cities. Overall, up to 100 other indigenous groups live in the rain forest in the east of the country, often in virtual isolation from civilisation, speaking traditional languages and surviving from hunting, fishing and agriculture. In between are the *mestizo* – people of mixed (mostly Spanish) and Native American background – forming the middle class of professionals, businessmen, military officers and government employees, making up to 37 per cent of the population. Only about 45 per cent of inhabitants of modern-day Peru are Native Americans, relatively few of them descending from the Inca. The remainder are of black African, Japanese or Chinese origin. Well over 70 per cent of the population now live in urban areas, principally along the coastal area that remains the economic centre of Peru.

Independence of Peru

The need to improve security after several uprisings in the 18th century, and to ease communication and trade with Spain, led to the split of the Viceroyalty of Peru and the creation of the viceroyalties of Nueva Granada and Rio de la Plata: these decisions in turn led to the formation of the majority of modern-day countries in South America. Indeed, while most of the continent was swept by wars of independence in the early 19th Century, Peru remained a royalist stronghold. The situation began to change only after military campaigns run by José de San Martin and Simón Bolívar in the 1810s. Together with Chilean General Bernardo O'Higgins, San Martin liberated large parts of Peru as a result of the battles of Chacabuco and Maipú in 1818, before – together with Thomas Cochrane, the British admiral and mercenary who commanded the Chilean navy – blockading Lima's port of Callao in 1820, and then settling to use diplomacy. Although negotiations failed, the Viceroy of Peru was then toppled by the very same general he appointed as commander-in-chief of the army responsible for the defence of the capital: San Martin quickly captured Lima and then declared Peruvian independence on 28 July 1821. With the help of Simon Bolívar's advance from the north, San Martin defeated the last royalist forces in the battles of Carabobo in 1821, and Pichincha a year later. Subsequently, Bolívar took over the task of fully liberating the country, San Martin retired from politics and the first parliament was assembled, which named Bolívar dictator of Peru and authorised him to organise a new military.

After enjoying a few decades of relative peace and stability, Peru sided with Bolivia during the five-year-long War of the Pacific against Chile, in the course of which it lost the department of Tarapacá in

1884. Subsequent internal struggles were settled during the rule of the Civilista Party, but this was toppled by the authoritarian regime imposed by Augusto B. Leguia, which in turn collapsed due to The Great Depression in 1932. Over the following three decades, the country was ruled by a coalition of the elite and the military.

The Coast, the Highlands and the Jungles of Ecuador

Earliest architectural remains of ancient civilisations in the area presently within the borders of Ecuador date back several thousands of years, and were probably related to the Maya civilisation of Central America. Quito, the present-day capital, is one of three cities in the Americas that precede the arrival of the Europeans (the other two are Mexico City, capital of the Aztec Empire, and Cuzco). Sadly, none of the earlier civilisations have left written records of their cultures, and thus it is only known that the original fortress was constructed as a centre of an ancient kingdom. This was first conquered by the Inca Empire in the late 15th Century, and then by the Spanish in 1532. While dominating the local tribes, the Inca fought back for years, proving a major obstacle to the invaders. Nevertheless, the Spanish were in the control of the area by 1534, and Pizarro appointed his brother, Gonzalo, the governor of Quito in 1540. Following Francisco's assassination, a short time later, Gonzalo Pizarro led a rebellion against Spain that lasted until 1548, when his forces were defeated by the Crown army at Jaquijaguana and he was executed.

Over the following centuries, the territory was administrated by the Viceroyalty of Peru – one of two major administrative divisions of 16th Century Spanish America – and became known under its modern-day name in around 1563. Geography dictated its division into four major regions, largely retained until today: the *Costa* (the coastal plain), the *Sierra* (central highlands), the *Oriente* (eastern jungle, covering about half of the country) and the Galápagos Islands. Although laying on the equator, due to varying elevation the country has a wide range of climates: the *Costa* is generally hot and humid, while the *Sierra* enjoys mild temperatures (depending on the elevation) and the *Oriente* is even warmer and more humid than the *Costa*. Forests have always represented an important resource: they still covered over 40 per cent of the country even in the late 20th century. Tropical jungles abound along the northern coast and within the inner portion of the southern coast, extending up the slopes of the Andes in some areas. Both flanks of the Cordilleras, and the *Oriente*, remain densely forested up to 3,050m (about 10,000ft). The wildlife varies, but large mammals include bears, jaguars and wildcats, while among the smaller are weasels, otters and skunk. Reptiles – including lizards, snakes and crocodiles – thrive on the slopes of the Andes and along the coastal lowlands. Despite Spanish colonisation, up to 80 per cent of the population remains composed of Native Americans and *mestizos*, while the remainder is equally divided between Europeans (mainly of Spanish descent) and Afro-Americans. The population of Ecuador was always predominantly urban, and even today, up to 50 per cent – largely Native Americans –live in the urban centres of the *Sierra*, while most other people reside in the *Costa*.

From 1717-23, Ecuador came under the presidency of the Viceroyalty of Nueva Granada in Bogotá, before being returned to the authority of the viceroy of Peru, and then in 1739 to Nueva Granada. A major revolt against colonial rule erupted in 1809, but was quickly suppressed. Similarly, the revolutionary government proclaimed in 1810 was removed by Spanish troops two years later. Nevertheless, the insurgents led by General Antonio José de Sucre – chief lieutenant of South American independence leader Simón Bolívar – continued their struggle and won final victory in 1822, when Ecuador became the 'Department of the South', a part of the confederacy known as the Republic of Colombia, or 'Gran Colombia', (which also included modern-day Venezuela, Panama and Colombia).

Ecuadorean Independence

After nearly 300 years of Spanish rule, the citizens of Quito were the first in Latin America to rebel and declare independence on 10 August 1809 (a day celebrated as Ecuador's Independence Day). Although this was suppressed by the Spanish military within 24 days, the efforts of the small city turned into a key milestone for the entire continent. Following protracted struggle, Guayaquil became the first city to gain enduring independence from Spain on 9 October 1820, and the rest of the country followed after rebels achieved victory at the Battle of Pichincha on 24 May 1822.

The subsequent history of Ecuador was dominated by a number of remarkable men: General José Maria Urbina, General Juan José Flores, Vicente Rocafuerte, Gabriel García Moreno and General Flavio Eloy Alfaro. Born in Venezuela, Flores was an officer in Bolívar's army during the War of Independence, commanding troops in Quito. When Bolívar left Ecuador, Flores took advantage of the growing anarchy in Gran Colombia to create his own government, and has ever since been known as the 'founder of the republic'. Educated in Europe, Rocafuerte was a member of Quito's upper class and a tolerant, progressive man of culture. Although considering him an enemy, Flores understood that Rocafuerte was the kind of man he needed in the government, and thus invited him to join. Starting in 1835, Rocafuerte gave Ecuador four remarkable years of administration, reforming the government, constructing hospitals and schools, and establishing friendly ties with all neighbouring countries. With their relations alternating between friendship and hostility, the partnership between Flores and Rocafuerte experienced a bitter end in 1845, when Flores was ousted and exiled in the course of a nationwide discontent. He fled to Spain and began to plot with Queen Isabella II to bring the west coast of South America back under Spanish rule. Before long, Ecuador's neighbours became so alarmed that during the Conference of Lima they began planning a mutual defence pact. With his plans foiled, Flores launched a new attempt in Guayaquil five years later with ships obtained from Peru, but received no welcome and departed for good.

The situation in Ecuador remained turbulent for many years. In 1851, General José Maria Urbina came to power through a *coup d'état*. He remained in the presidency until 1856, and then continued dominating the political scene until 1860. The power struggle between Urbina and his archrival, García Moreno, was to determine the dichotomy between the Liberals in Guayaquil and Conservatives from Quito that dominated the political scene in Ecuador for the next 100 years.

Differences between Liberals and Conservatives reached the state of a near-civil war in 1859, known in the country as 'the Terrible Year'. Local *caudillos* (leaders) had declared several regions autonomous of the central government, and one of them ceded the southern provinces of Ecuador to an occupying Peruvian army. This act proved outrageous enough to unite diverse previously disparate elements. García Moreno, a staunch Conservative, thus put aside his projects to place Ecuador under a French protectorate and his differences with Flores, established himself in power and then launched a campaign of putting down local rebellions and forcing out the Peruvians. The final push of this effort was the defeat of the Peruvian-backed forces at the Battle of Guayaquil, which overturned the Treaty of Mapasingue and opened the way for García Moreno establishing himself in power. During his presidency that lasted until 1875, Moreno favoured administrative reforms, modernisation of agriculture, road construction and, above all, the development of a school system under the complete control of the Catholic clergy. Although assassinated in 1875, he secured two additional decades of Conservative rule, first under the dictatorship of General Ignacio de Vientimilla y Villacís and then under two successive civilian governments. It was during this period that the demand for products such as coffee made Ecuador generally prosperous.

In 1895, the Liberals seized power in a coup led by their strongman, Eloy Alfaro. Although succeeded by another Liberal general in 1901, Alfaro remained influential and returned to power in 1906. During the following years, he put into effect the essential points of the Liberal programme – including the elimination of the privileged legal position of the Roman Catholic Church, establishment of a system of public education and construction of the crucial railroad between Guayaquil and Quito. However, Alfaro was overthrown in 1911 and the country was thrown into a 50-year-long period of economic and political instability. A crucial reason for this was that bananas had become a major export crop in the 1920s, and the collapse of world markets during the Great Depression of the 1930s dealt the country a very hard blow.

Border Dispute

The background to the border-conflict between Ecuador and Peru can be traced back to the early 18th Century, when the Spanish were distributing the former Inca Empire between different *Audiencias* (courts exercising military, political and judicial power) and viceroyalties they established. Because of the poor geographical knowledge of the area in question, the *Real Cédulas* (royal decrees issued by the Spanish Crown) separated many of the colonial-era administrations by poorly defined borders, and these haphazard territorial definitions subsequently led to numerous border disputes among new South American nations.

Ecuador was originally constituted under the Viceroyalty of Peru under the name of the '*Real Audiencia de Quito*'. In 1739, it was incorporated into the Viceroyalty of Nueva Granada. After the Battle of Pichincha – fought on 24 May 1822 between the Patriot army under General José de Sucre and the Spanish Royalist army commanded by Field Marshal Melchor Aymerich, and won by the former – the territories of Guayaquil and the *Audiencia* of Quito were incorporated as part of Gran Colombia. Looking for economic compensation from the Peruvian government, Bolívar made claims for the Peruvian territories of Tumbes, Jaen and Maynas, which were refused, with the explanation that splitting them away would represent a 'mutilation of territories' and would be against the *Uti Possidetis* principle, which is to say, it would no longer respect which parts of the country were occupied by each party as in 1810.[1]

Icaza-Pritchett Treaty

The resulting impasse was temporarily settled by the consecutive treaties of Girón and Guayaquil, and then the signing of the Pedemonte-Mosquera Protocol. Nevertheless, the situation remained tense even after the dissolution of Gran Colombia and the creation of the Republic of Ecuador in 1830. As so often, the principal reasons were land – and money. Control over the northern part of what is nowadays the Loreto region in Peru was hotly disputed by Ecuador, resulting in repeated quarrels. Moreover, during the war of independence, the government of Gran Colombia had incurred a number of debts to private European creditors. The three daughter states then split the debts among themselves, with Ecuador assuming responsibility for 21.5 per cent.[2] As Ecuador failed to pay its dues, a committee of holders of Latin American bonds organised itself and sent several emissaries to Quito to arrange a settlement. Related negotiations led to a treaty between George S. Pritchett, representative of the Ecuadorean Land Company Ltd, and Ecuadorean Minister of Finance Don Francisco de Paula Icaza, that gave the creditors rights to several territories in Esmeraldas, some on the shores of the Zamora River, a large section in the canton of Canelos and an even larger portion near the Canar River. The agreement stipulated that Ecuadorean sovereignty would be preserved, but all activities carried out there would be tax-exempt for 15 years.[3]

Ownership of several of the territories in question was hotly disputed by Peru, the government of which sent a letter of protest over the signing of the Icaza-Pritchett Treaty to the Ecuadorean Minister of Foreign Relations, Antonio Mata. In November 1857, the Peruvian Resident Minister to Ecuador, Juan Celestino Cavero, had arrived in Quito seeking to resolve the dispute. He promptly called for the treaty to be declared void because the territories in Canelos belonged to Peru based on a *Real Cédula* of 1802 and the *Uti Pssidetis* posture adopted by Peru in 1810. Arguing that the *Real Cédula* of 1802 did not transfer territorial rights to the Viceroyalty of Peru because it was never authorised by the Viceroy of Santa Fe (meaning that the ownership of territories according to Spanish law remained as it was before 1802), Mata declared the *Uti Possidetis* principle void. As the two countries continued the diplomatic correspondence, the resulting 'paper war' was continued until 29 July 1858, when Mata requested that Cavero be expelled. In turn, Cavero complained about what he considered multiple transgressions carried out by the Ecuadorean government and press against Peru's honour. Quito then severed its relations with Peru and expelled Cavero. In retaliation for this act, on 26 October 1858, the Peruvian Congress authorised President Ramón Castilla to command an army against Ecuador to secure the national territory against its sale to British creditors, and to impose a blockade of Ecuador's ports. The blockade began in earnest on 4 November 1858, following arrival of the first Peruvian Navy warship – the frigate BAP *Amazonas* – in Ecuadorean waters, and was run by Rear Admiral Ignacio Mariátegui.[4]

Ecuadorean Civil War of 1859-60

Facing the Peruvian blockade, Ecuadorean President Francisco Robles moved the national capital to Guayaquil and ordered General José María Urbina to defend it. This decision proved highly unpopular and provoked the emergence of several armed opposition groups – nearly all championed by regional *caudillos*. While Gabriel García Moreno reacted by quickly setting up a provisional government seated in Quito, and Guayaquil's General Guillermo Franco declaring himself Supreme Chief of the Guayas, the country was further split among a number of *Jefaturas Supremas* (Supreme Commands). In turn, Franco was recognised as the new president of Ecuador by Peruvian President Ramón Castilla, who – in hope of brokering a favourable territorial deal – continued maintaining the blockade of the Gulf of Guayaquil.

In mid-May 1859, General Urbina set out for Quito to subdue García Moreno and his movement, the forces of the provisional government proving no match for his and the capital falling in June. After fleeing to Peru, García Moreno requested help from President Castilla, and the Peruvian leader agreed to supply him with 3,000 rifles, ammunition, uniforms and boots. Convinced he would now act with the full support of Peru, García Moreno published a manifesto for his countrymen in July 1859, instructing them to accept Peru as their ally against Robles, despite the territorial dispute and blockade, and then travelled to Guayaquil to meet General Franco, who agreed to support him. However, on 31 August 1859, Castilla betrayed his commitment to García Moreno and instead agreed to support Franco

and end the blockade of the Gulf of Guayaquil. In return, Franco agreed to the so-called Mosquera-Zelaya Protocol, under which Peru was to take control of Ecuador.[5]

Disavowing this treaty, Robles reacted by moving the capital to Riobamba, where he handed the leadership of the government to Jerónimo Carrión before leaving the country together with General Urvina. Meanwhile, Rafael Carvajal, a member of the defeated provisional government, led a sizeable military force to invade Ecuador and establish a new provisional government in Quito. Amid the resulting anarchy and general tumult, Castilla continued seeking for ways to impose a favourable border settlement. On 20 September 1859, he declared his support for the new government in Quito and then launched an amphibious invasion from Callao. The Peruvian force arrived in Guayaquil on 4 October, where Castilla arranged for successive meetings with Franco and García Moreno. However, when the latter heard about the Peruvian's meeting with Franco, he broke off further negotiations. After convincing Franco that he would fulfil his promises, Castilla landed his 5,000 troops in Ecuador and they set up a camp near the *hacienda* of Mapasingue, outside Guayaquil.

El Traidor

This act prompted four major Ecuadorean leaders to unite, despite their mutual differences. However, instead of launching a counterattack, they first agreed to delegate to Franco the task of negotiating with Peru on condition of Guayaquil and Cuenca not pledging to annex, cede or assign to any government any part of Ecuadorean territory under any pretext or name. However, Franco negotiated just such a treaty with Castilla, and the two signed the Treaty of Mapasingue on 25 January 1860. Under that agreement, the territorial debate was to be solved once and forever – to Peruvian advantage. The treaty declared the Icaza-Pritchett agreement null and void, accepted Peru's position

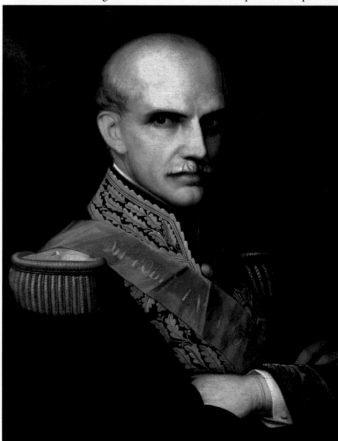

Dr Gabriel García Moreno, leader of the provisional government of Quito. (*Presidencia de la República del Ecuador*)

Marshal Ramón Castilla y Marquezado, President of Peru during the Ecuadorean Civil War of 1859-1860. (Military Museum of Peru)

The War of the Pacific

Over the following years, Peru became embroiled in multiple border disputes with various of its neighbours. Bolivia and Chile first negotiated their Boundary Treaty (also known as the Treaty of Mutual Benefits) in 1866, but then Bolivia entered an alliance with Peru and Argentina against Chile in February 1873. Chile was then devastated by an economic crisis and began looking for a replacement for its silver, copper and wheat exports. Aiming to capture additional mineral sources, owners of the Chilean nitrate companies then 'bulldozed' President Anibal Pinto into declaring war on Bolivia.[6]

In February 1879, the Chilean government deployed 200 troops to land in the port city of Antofagasta, with orders to occupy the area south of the 23rd Parallel. After Peruvian mediation attempts failed, Bolivia declared war on Chile in late February, although this was not immediately announced. On 23 March 1879, Chilean troops and cavalry defeated the Bolivians in the Battle of Topáter, thus starting an armed conflict. Although neither party was prepared for war – whether financially or militarily (the entire Chilean military totalled about 2,400, that of Peru about 5,500, while Bolivia was suffering from famine) – the conflict was intensified over the following months, with both Chile and Peru seeking to control the coast along the nearly waterless and largely unpopulated Atacama Desert. Early on, Chile blockaded the Peruvian port of Iquique, starting in April 1879, provoking a number of naval clashes. While initially successfully fighting back, the Peruvian navy was gradually reduced, and from October-November the same year played no more active role in the fighting. Once in possession of naval supremacy, Chile launched a series of four land campaigns that successively occupied Tarapacá and Arica-Tacna, then ransacked the capital of Lima and – in 1882 – destroyed Peruvian resistance in the *sierra*. Realising that the five-year-long and utterly devastating war had to be brought to an end or the country would be completely ruined, in April 1882 the Peruvian government called for peace. Hostilities between Chile and Peru were formally concluded on 20 October 1883, and those between Bolivia and Chile in 1884. While related negotiations went on until 1929, Bolivia and Peru were eventually forced into accepting the loss of entire provinces, including some major sources of mineral wealth. During the following decades, successive governments in Lima remained preoccupied with numerous social and economic reforms aimed at recovering from the war's damage. Political stability in the country was thus achieved only in the early 1900s.

Turbulent 1930s

As the 20th Century began, Peru was thus still in dispute with three of its five neighbours: with Ecuador and Colombia to the north and north-east, and with Chile to the south. Despite prolonged negotiations, tensions were further heightened by minor military actions. In 1911, an armed incident between Peruvian and Colombian armies in the town of La Pedrera – a small outpost located in the north-western Putumayo – led as a consequence to the demilitarisation of the area between the Caquetá and Putumayo rivers, as well as the establishment of an uncomfortable *modus vivendi* over these territories. This situation changed on 24 March 1922, when, with the intention of once and for all settling the border dispute with Colombia (and, subsequently, with Ecuador), Peruvian President Augusto Bernardino Leguía authorised the signing of the United States-backed Salomon-Lozano Treaty, by which Peru granted Colombia sovereignty over the territories between the Caquetá and Putumayo rivers, as well as an adjacent territorial fringe – known as the Amazon Trapeze.[7]

The Salomon-Lozano Treaty gave Colombia a long-dreamed of and coveted access to the Amazon River. In exchange, Colombia

of *Uti Possidetis* and allowed Ecuador two years to substantiate its ownership of Quijos and Canelos or accept Peru's rights – thus *de-facto* acknowledging the *Real Cédula* of 1802. Castilla and his troops then embarked and sailed for Peru on 10 February 1860.

Becoming aware of the treasonous pact, the disparate governments of Ecuador quickly united against their common enemy: *El Traidor* – the traitor – Franco. Led by Juan José Flores and García Moreno, they launched an advance on Guayaquil. By accident, this happened as Castilla found himself facing widespread domestic protest and a border dispute with Bolivia. Thus, while Franco was supported by forces under the command of his brother, Juan José, his troops were overpowered and forced to retreat. The decisive battle took place between 22 and 24 September 1860 when Guayaquil quickly fell to Flores' and García Moreno's men, while Franco's troops fled in disarray, many drowning while trying to reach the last few Peruvian ships still in the harbour. Ashamed by his defeat, Franco never returned to Ecuador: he died in exile in Callao, Peru, in 1873.

The Ecuadorean Congress nullified the Treaty of Mapasingue in 1861; the Peruvian Congress followed in fashion two years later, and the two governments then agreed to return to the status of *casus belli*. However, with the entire affair producing no favourable results for Peru, the territorial dispute remained unresolved.

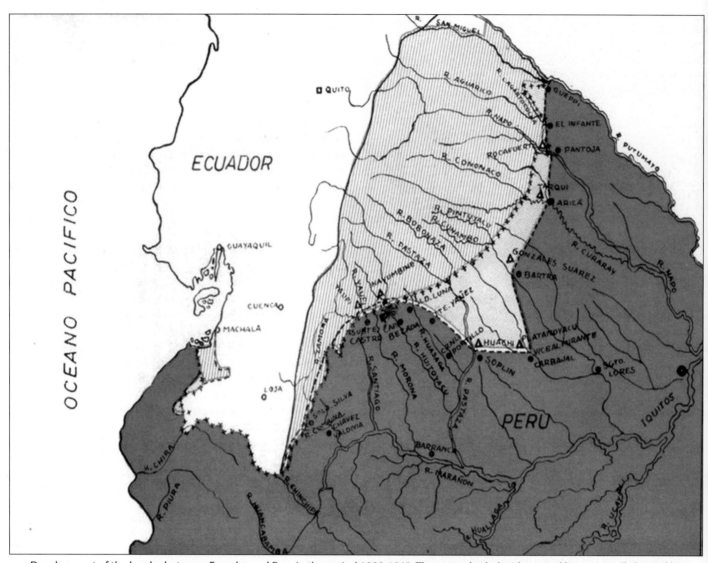

Development of the border between Ecuador and Peru in the period 1889-1942. The areas shaded with vertical lines were all claimed by Peru on basis of the *Real Cédula* of 1802. The Status Quo Line, marked with small crosses, and – since the Rio de Janeiro Protocol of 1942 – has been accepted as the international border. Areas south and east of the Status Quo Line were claimed by Ecuador. (IEHAP via author)

recognised as Peruvian the previously disputed territories south of the Putumayo and handed over the so-called '*Triangulo de Sucumbios*', a small but strategic territory between the Putumayo and San Miguel rivers in the north-western corner of the Amazon rain forest. What may have seemed strange to many Peruvians – perhaps because of the conspicuous silence kept by Leguía's political enemies regarding this matter – was the fact that such a territorial exchange allowed Peru to 'block' Ecuador in its pretensions towards the Amazon, and would eventually allow for the signing of agreements favourable to Peruvian interests. Consequently, the territorial concessions gave Colombia a harbour and free navigation on the Amazon, whilst Peru obtained a strategic victory in its objective to set concrete demarcation of the north and north-eastern borders. More importantly, the treaty pleased the United States Government, which had interest in providing some kind of compensation to Colombia after its loss of Panama: Leguía, who was well-liked by the Americans, thus secured US support for the upcoming round of negotiations with Chile for the return of the occupied territories of Tacna, Arica and Tarata.

However, the application of this treaty hurt the economy of the Caucheros, powerful landowners in Iquitos who profited from the harvest of the natural rubber extracted from the Caucho plants in the Putumayo, turning them into fierce opponents. Using their economic power, the Caucheros virtually bought the public consciousness through paying for related advertisements in the principal newspapers

and radio stations of Lima. These were used to launch a campaign against President Leguía, accusing him of treason. The result was a widespread social unrest and, ultimately, the *coup d'état* and later imprisonment of the president, which ended with his death on 6 February 1932.

Between September 1932 and May 1933, Peru became embroiled in a short-lived armed conflict with Colombia over territory in the Amazon Basin, the so-called 'Leticia Incident'. A wider war was averted through an agreement for Colombia to take one part of this territory and Peru another, with negotiations resulting in an agreement that actually favoured the Peruvians since it froze the Colombian border once and for all, while strengthening the – until then – somewhat precarious Peruvian position in the western Amazon. This perhaps explains the strong reaction by part of the Ecuadorean government that, after gaining knowledge of the agreement, accused Colombia of treason and vowed not to recognise the validity of the arrangements between its two neighbours.

Overall, the relationship between Peru and Ecuador progressively deteriorated during the second half of the 1930s. In 1936, after a series of border frictions and incidents, the situation seemed to normalise when both governments reached an agreement to respect their current territorial possessions. According to this *Status Quo* Treaty, each country would maintain its sovereignty upon territories occupied *de facto* at the time of the agreement's signature, committing to mutually respect the border situation until a definitive frontier agreement was reached. However, continuous political instability affected Ecuador: indeed, the treaty was doomed to fail after President Federico Paez was overthrown. The five successive administrations took an even more intransigent and antagonist position towards Peru, gradually worsening the diplomatic relationship between the two countries.

This situation nearly developed into armed conflict in 1938 when Ecuadorean troops occupied the Noblecilla and Matapalo islands, which were claimed by Peru as part of its territories. This occupation was only put an end to after the issue of an ultimatum to Quito by Peruvian chancellery.

2
PERUVIAN MILITARY BUILD-UP

The need to protect the northern frontier from the ever-growing animosity displayed by Ecuador led the Peruvian government, headed by General Oscar R. Benavides, to consider the use of force against its neighbour as a last resort in order to force it into accepting the definitive border agreement – on favourable terms, of course. With this objective in mind, Benavides had launched an aggressive modernisation programme for the armed forces and, between 1933 and 1939, the air force alone had received more than 50 new training and combat aircraft, opened new airbases and improved training and organisation with the arrival of an Italian military mission.

Military of Peru
While some militia units existed earlier, the *Ejército del Perú* (EP, Peruvian Army) was officially established on 18 August 1821 in the form of the *Legión Peruana de la Guardia* (Peruvian Guard Legion), which was one of the key participants in the final campaign against

Spanish rule in South America, led by Simon Bolívar. Lack of solid political institutions resulted in every Peruvian president until 1872 holding a military rank. The military also had a major role in the definition of national borders through the wars against Gran Colombia, the Peru-Bolivian Confederacy, two invasions of Bolivia and the Ecuadorean Civil War, after which it was significantly expanded and modernised. Indeed, continuous overspending for the military resulted in a major fiscal crisis that severely weakened the army and was followed by defeat in the War of the Pacific. It was only after the arrival of a French military mission in 1896 that the situation began to change. By 1900, the peacetime strength of the armed forces was increased to six infantry battalions with about 2,000 troops, two cavalry regiments of around 700 troops and one artillery regiment with around 500 men. Still under French guidance, the Peruvian Army underwent numerous reforms through the early 20th Century, when the *Escuela Superior de Guerra* (War College) was established and the

Between late 1938 and early 1939, the Peruvian army took delivery of a total of 24 Czech ČKD LTL light tanks. Organized into two companies, 12 of these saw service during the 1941 campaign, all under the command of the TON. (Amaru Tincopa Gallegos Collection)

Peruvian doctrine was influenced by the French military mission operating in Peru at the time, and emphasised the use of tanks in support of infantry attacks rather than in independent mobile columns. For example, on 25 and 26 July 1941, Peruvian troops supported by LTP tanks pushed through the Zarumilla area and captured the villages of Carcabón, Huabillos and Balsalito from Ecuador in rapid actions, proving unstoppable thanks to their new weapons. (Amaru Tincopa Gallegos Collection)

A Praha T-6 tractor negotiates the Zarumilla River during operations against the Ecuadorians. These tractors were found to be extremely helpful in towing trucks across the large rivers found on the border. (Amaru Tincopa Gallegos Collection)

Peruvian Army personnel belonging to the *Batallón de Carros de Combate No.1* based at the Barbones fort in Lima, prior to the deployment of the 12 LTP tanks and support units to the northern frontier. (Amaru Tincopa Gallegos Collection)

country divided into four military regions. General professionalisation resulted in the Army's good performance in clashes with Colombia in 1911 and 1932, and then the war with Ecuador in 1941.

The *Marina de Guerra del Perú* (MGP, Peruvian Navy) was officially established on 8 October 1821 and successfully operated against the Spanish during the War of Independence (1821-24), by when it also included the Peruvian Naval Infantry. Its growth was impacted by the same economic crisis of the 1870s that had such a negative influence upon the Army, and thus the Navy was caught unprepared by the outbreak of the War of the Pacific. The MGP was thereafter rebuilt from the ground up, and by the early 20th Century included one cruiser, seven screw-driven steamers and 10 other ships. It was reinforced through the acquisition of scout cruisers *Almirante Grau* and *Coronel Bolognesi* in 1907, followed by its first two submarines.

Cuerpo Aeronáutico del Perú

The history of the military aviation in Peru began on the morning of 2 December 1915, when EP Captain Juan E. O'Connor took off aboard a Bleriot XI monoplane from a small airfield in Bellavista to carry out a tactical observation of manoeuvres held by the army in San Juan de Miraflores district on the outskirts of the capital. This flight, unprecedented in Peruvian military history, marked the first use of aviation by Peruvian armed forces. After completing his flight, O'Connor issued a thorough report to his superiors, detailing his impressions and recommendations for the future employment of aviation. Consequently, the High Command of the Armed Forces authorised the beginning of preliminary studies for the creation of the Peruvian Army Aviation component, which were completed by mid-1916.

In June of 1916, with the aim of forming a core of competent aviators, the EP decided to send two of its more outstanding officers on an instructional tour to El Palomar military aviation school in Buenos Aires, Argentina. However, following long bureaucratic delays, Lieutenants Enrique Ruiz Espinoza and Guillermo Protzel del Castillo did not arrive in Buenos Aires until the beginning of 1918, commencing their training immediately. Unfortunately, shortly after the beginning of their training, Lieutenant Ruiz Espinoza was killed in a flight accident when, at 1700 hours on 13 May 1918, the Bleriot XI monoplane he was flying crashed at El Palomar airfield in Argentina. Far from being discouraged by this tragedy, his comrades Lieutenant Guillermo Protzel del Castillo and Peruvian civilians Enrique Parodi and Manuel Sanchez, who had arrived at El Palomar shortly after with their own funds, successfully managed to complete their flight training and returned to Peru by mid-November of that year. With them was a Henri Farman biplane, a donation from Peruvian residents in Buenos Aires, which was christened *Teniente Ruiz* in honour of the fallen Peruvian aviator. In January 1919, Lieutenant Protzel used this aircraft to resume flights in Peru and was followed shortly thereafter by Midshipman Ismael Montoya, who in July 1919 also graduated from El Palomar flight school.

Army Aviation Service

The Peruvian military aviation service was officially born with the issue of a Supreme Decree by President Jose Luis Pardo y Barreda dated 28 January 1919 which created the *Servicio de Aviación del Ejército* (SAE, Army Aviation Service) under the following guidelines:

North American NA-50 fighter-bombers from the *41 Escuadrilla del XXI Escuadrón de Caza* in Chiclayo during early 1941. Five of these aircraft were assigned to the unit and took active part during the conflict. (IEHAP)

Five Caproni Ca.135 Tipo Perú medium bombers during a display at Teniente Coronel Pedro Ruiz Gallo air base in 1940. The CAP ceased using these aircraft against Ecuadorian targets, employing them in transport and reconnaissance missions instead. An engine malfunction caused the loss of one of these big and underpowered bombers while returning from a reconnaissance mission on 10 July. (IEHAP)

Some of the aircraft assigned under the command of the *Primer Grupo Aéreo*. A total of 10 Caproni Ca.310 *Libeccios*, three Ca.135s, six Ca.114s and two Ca.111s can be seen in this picture, taken in Chiclayo in late June 1941. (IEHAP)

THE PRESIDENT OF THE REPUBLIC, considering:

1. – That an Army Aviation Service will constitute an indispensable institutional entity for the national defence;

2. – That, at the time it is not possible to organise this service as autonomous entity, but only as a branch of the army;

3. – Therefore, it is a requirement for the future organisation of the service to train the personnel which would serve as the foundations for its definitive organisation; and,

4. – Having reviewed the project prepared by the Army's Engineer Corps Direction:

DECREES:

Art.1 – To create the "*Servicio de Aviación del Ejército*", which should: a) perform the study, acquisition and maintenance of aeronautical machines; b) administrate, instruct and mobilise all personnel linked to the service of such machines.

Art.2. – At the time, the only operational section will be the *Centro de Aviación* [Aviation Centre], to be located in Lima, with the aim to create similar units within each military region.

Art.3. – Each "*Centro de Aviación*" will act as a training school for future aviators and will provide, in the event of mobilisation, air units or squadrons.

Art.4. – Each Air Squadron shall comprise:

a) Material. – 4 or 6 aircraft organised in two or three sections; a ground support unit with a number of indispensable vehicles allowing optimal operation of the unit (tractors,

A portrait of the original members of the *41 Escuadrilla de Caza* during a visit to Las Palmas in January 1941. First from the right is the young Lieutenant José Abelardo Quiñones Gonzales, who went missing in action during an attack on Ecuadorian positions on 23 July. (Amaru Tincopa Gallegos Collection)

Aerial view of Teniente Coronel Pedro Ruiz Gallo air base facilities in Chiclayo. Its proximity to the area of operations made this base an ideal supply and maintenance operations centre for the aircraft assigned to the TON. (Amaru Tincopa Gallegos Collection)

Aerial view of the advanced field of Talara. Note the four Fairey Fox aircraft stationed temporarily at the base during their transfer from Lima to Tumbes. (Amaru Tincopa Gallegos Collection)

21 trainers, five Curtiss H2L flying boats, four Douglas DT-2B bombers and a pair of Change-Vought OU-1A Corsair observation biplanes.

Unification: Birth of the *Cuerpo de Aviación del Perú*

During their first years, both the SAE and CAN hired several foreign military missions to improve the training of its students as well as to help with the organisation of the incipient services in order to turn them into effective combat forces. Invariably, the arrival of each mission also meant the arrival of new aircraft for their respective ranks. In the case of the SAE, French and British missions were followed, albeit very briefly, by a German team of advisors, while the CAN opted to hire the services of a US Navy mission which, from 1923 until the end of the 1920s provided organisation and instruction for the naval aviators. All of the missions that arrived in Peru were composed of experienced aviators, which helped pave the way for the first promotions of local aviators as well as improving the organisation and doctrine of use of these incipient aerial forces.

However, the constant introduction of new types into service without following any kind of acquisition procedures soon resulted in the military aviation facing a logistical nightmare, leading to a waste of resources considered unacceptable for a Third World country like Peru. Therefore, during the second half of the 1920s, the government launched the first studies towards the unification of the two aerial services, an idea that eventually came to fruition with the creation, by means of Law No.6511, of the *Ministerio de Marina y Aviación* (MMA, Navy and Aviation Ministry).[1]

This was the first step undertaken to achieve the unification of the country's existing military aviation services, providing the necessary legal frame for the merger of the SAE and CAN under a single command structure, a lengthy process that ended nearly four years later with the promulgation, on 3 July 1932, of a Supreme Decree giving birth to the *Cuerpo de Aviación del Perú* (CAP, Peruvian Aviation Corps).

The creation of the CAP responded to the need to maximise the use of resources available to the pre-existing aviation services under a single, unified command in order to obtain the inherent benefits of simplified logistics and reduction in maintenance costs and workload, as well as to improve future acquisition processes under modern, up-to-date parameters.

The so-called Putumayo conflict between early September 1932 and late May 1933 caught the CAP in the middle of the consolidation process, and the outcome of operations, during which the Peruvians lost nearly 30 per cent of their aircraft strength, evidenced the need for additional changes to be made to the CAP structure, doctrine and organisation. Therefore, on 13 October 1936, the MMA issued a Supreme Decree approving a secret package of regulations known as the *Estrategia y Logística del CAP* (Aeronautics Corps Logistics and Strategy). The promulgation of this document marked a breakthrough in the development of Peruvian military aviation as it made possible the execution of regulations established in Supreme Resolution No.93 which introduced a number of dispositions regarding the

truck-shops and automobiles for liaison duties, wireless telegraph, etc.).

b) Personnel. – An aviation company whose composition will be established separately.

Art.5. – Once established, all centres will become dependent of the *Alta Dirección de Aeronáutica* [High Aeronautic Bureau] comprising a High Command and a General Staff, with several units under their command including the maintenance station, on the front line.

Published in Lima on January 28, 1919.

Signed: José Pardo y Barreda   José Juan Manuel Zuloaga

Following its foundation, the SAE initially operated from the Bellavista airfield, flying a mixture of French and British types such as Avro 504Ks, Caudron G.3s, Salmson 2A.2s and Bristol F.2bs. Shortly thereafter, in May 1919, the incipient air service moved its operations to Maranga airfield, where a proper aerial instruction school had been established as the *Centro de Aviación Militar* (Military Aviation Centre). By 1922, however, Maranga airfield was deemed to be too small to sustain the increased pace of operations and, therefore, the Army sought a new location for its operations. This was finally found in the form of a large state farm known as *Las Palmas*, located south of Lima, and in July 1922 an aerodrome along with buildings for the newly established *Escuela Central de Aviación Militar* (Central Military Aviation School) were opened there.

Naval Aviation Corps

Shortly after the creation of the army aviation, the MGP also got its own aviation service with the issuing of a Supreme Decree dated 26 January 1920, which created the *Cuerpo de Aviación Naval* (CAN, Naval Aviation Corps), which was put under the command of *Capitan de Fragata* Juan Leguia Swayne, president Leguia's son. First operating from a small base on San Lorenzo Island off Lima, the CAN operations were soon moved to Ancón bay, located about 30 miles north of Lima, where a seaplane base and training centre for naval aviators were established. Among the first aircraft assigned to the new-born service were a pair of Norman-Thompson NT-2Bs, six Curtiss model F Seagulls and a trio of Georges-Levy GL.40B.2s. After the reorganisation of the naval services, the CAN was put under the command of Harold B. Grow, an experienced United States Navy officer, and re-equipped with new aircraft including five Boeing model

Table 1: Standard organisational structure of Air Groups of the CAP	
Purpose	**Unit Element**
Air Group	
administration	Air Group HQ
executive	2nd HQ
tactical elements	*escuadrones* (squadrons)
technical elements	technical services
other administrative elements	engineering, personnel, maintenance, administrative and transport department (for each squadron)
Squadron	
tactical	flights and patrols
logistical	departments, sections and divisions
technical	instruction groups (like EAM's four instruction *escadrilles*)
Squadron's material and logistic structure	
Flying Echelon	flight material and crews required for specific operation
Ground Echelon	ground crews and equipment required to provide support to flying elements

Men and machines from the *XI Escuadrón de Bombardeo* and *XXI Escuadrón de Caza* parked during a review held at Teniente Coronel Pedro Ruiz Gallo air base on 9 April 1941 after completing operational exercises. (Amaru Tincopa Gallegos Collection)

Tumbes forward base, July 1941. Fighter, liaison and transport aircraft assigned to the various CAP units that deployed to this field during the first days of the conflict. (Amaru Tincopa Gallegos Collection)

administration, structure and operations of the air force, including the change of the air force denomination *from Cuerpo de Aviación del Perú* to *Cuerpo Aeronáutico del Perú* (Peruvian Aeronautical Corps). A detailed description of the typical air group and squadron structure according to the new CAP regulations is presented in Table 1.[2]

The regulations also established the *Comandancia General de Aeronáutica* (CGA, General Air Command) as an entity subordinated to the MMA, enjoying the following powers and functions:

(a)   To ensure proper preparation and growth of all CAP members, as well as to maintain discipline throughout its structure and ranks.

(b)   To serve as an administrative and technical advisor to the MMA Secretary, providing him with advice on technical matters when required.

To accomplish these functions, the CGA had the following structure and resources at its disposal:

(a)   For tactical and strategic matters: High Staff of Aeronautics.

(b)   For technical and logistic matters: Directorate of Technical Services; Directorate for Commercial and Civil Aviation; Directorate for Civil Constructions; Directorate for Aeronautic Personnel; Directorate for Supplies and Accountability; Directorate for Health Services.

(c)   For immediate advice and consulting: Aeronautics Consulting Council; Physical Capacity Investigation Council; Economics Council; Investigation for Superior and Subordinate Officers Council.

(d)   Aeronautical instruction centres: *Escuela de Bombardeo, Armamento y Tiro Aéreo* (Bombing, Weaponry and Air Gunnery School); *Escuela de Aviación Militar* (Military Aviation School); *Escuela de Entrenamiento en Hidroaviones* (Seaplane Training School); *Escuela de Vuelo en Altura* (High Altitude Flight School).

Additionally, studies began for the future implementation of the following instruction centres:

(a) *Escuela Superior de Aeronáutica* (Aeronautics Superior Studies School).

(b) *Escuela de Sub Oficiales* (Sub-Officers School).

New Air Bases and Auxiliary Airfields

Along with the expansion and reorganisation of the Peruvian military aviation, a large number of airfields were constructed across Peru between 1934 and 1936, as listed in Table 2.

As the air force grew in organisation and presence across Peruvian territory, measures were also taken by the high command to allow it to keep pace with the fast technological advances of aviation during the decade. As part of these measures, the CAP launched a new modernisation programme in 1938 aimed at replacing certain types that – despite having been purchased only a few years previously – were approaching obsolescence (such as the Nieuport-Delage NiD-121 and Potez 390), as well as incorporating new types intended to accomplish specific missions following the analysis of events taking place in Europe. Accordingly, during 1938 the Peruvian government signed a number of contracts for the purchase of seven North American NA-50 fighter-bombers, 16 Caproni Ca.310 *Libeccio* light bombers, 10 Douglas 8A-3P attack aircraft and four Grumman G-21 Goose amphibious aircraft, all of which would be delivered during the first half of 1939.

In the meantime, increasing frictions between Ecuadorean

Another view of Tumbes forward airfield. A single Grumman G-21 Goose from *84 Escuadrilla* can be seen between a pair of Caproni Ca.111 transports from *105 Escuadrilla de Transporte*. (IEHAP)

and Peruvian police and army units across the border continued to erode relations between the countries. While the Peruvians expected to eventually find a diplomatic way out of the border crisis, in 1936 the hard line government led by President General Oscar Raimundo Benavides ordered the armed forces high command to organise a "pacification plan" for the northern frontier, aimed at the neutralisation of Ecuadorean armed forces in the border as a final resort to the frontier dispute.

Northern and North-Eastern Operations Theatres

Despite the success of Benavides' administration in economy and infrastructure-related development, his government found itself exposed to increasing pressure at home and from abroad. As a fascist sympathiser with strong ties to the Mussolini government, he was

Table 2: Air Bases in Peru, 1934-41

Divison and Sector	Designation
Air Region North	
Main Air Base	Teniente Coronel Pedro Ruiz Gallo (Chichlayo, Lambayeque)
Forward Bases	Tumbes, Ayabaca, Piura
Liaison Bases	Paita, Piura, Huancabamba, Cajamarca, Chimbote (Las Zorras), Ancash
Air Region Centre	
Main Air Base	Las Palmas (Lima)
Secondary Bases	El Tablazo (Lima), San Ramon (Junin), Huancayo (Huancayo)
Liaison Airfields	Pisco, Ica
Auxiliary Airfields	Villa, Chilca (both in the Lima area)
Air Region East	
Main Air Base	Teniente Gustavo Cornejo (Iquitos)
Secondary Bases	Pucallpa, Ucayali
Forward Bases and Seaplane Bases	Güepi (Loreto), Pantoja (Loreto), Ramón Castilla (Loreto), Puerto Maldonado (Madre de Dios)
Liaison Airfields and Seaplane Bases	Bellavista (Meranón River), Barranca, Tepestad, Requena, Dos de Mayo, Contamana, Puerto Victoria, Puerto Bermúdez, Cumaria, Atalaya (Madre de Dios), Masisea
Air Region South	
Main Air Base	Mayor Guillermo Protzel del Castillo (Vitor)
Secondary Air Bases	Juliaca, Puno
Forward Air Bases	Tacna, Huancané
Liaison Airfields	Puerto Inca (Arequipa), Cusco, Matarani (Arequipa), Ayacucho, Ilo (Moquegua)
Maritime Front	(seaplane bases)
Main Air Base	Alfrez Huguet (Ancón)
Forward Airfields	Chimbote Bay (Ancash), Puerto Pizarro (Tumbes), Paracas (Ica), Mollendo

Chiclayo, June 1941. The human and material complement of the *XI Escuadrón de Bombardeo* crowd the ramp at Teniente Coronel Pedro Ruiz Gallo air base after the squadron received orders to prepare to deploy to the forward bases near the border. (Amaru Tincopa Gallegos Collection)

Chiclayo, 4 July 1941. Captain Fernando Parraud and a number of unidentified civilians next to XXI-41-1, the aircraft assigned to the commanding officer of the *41 Escadrille*, *XXI Escuadrón de Caza*, shortly before departing for Tumbes forward airfield. (Ines de Pierola Collection)

North American NA-50 serial XXI-41-2 and its pilot Lieutenant Renán Elías Olivera seen during a review in Tumbes on the morning of 6 July 1941. Elias tragically died the next day when a bomb he was trying to detach from his aircraft detonated while still on its rack, destroying the plane. (Amaru Tincopa Gallegos Collection)

in power with the help of the Congress for an additional three-year mandate. Indeed, there is little doubt that during the second half of his tenure, Benavides actually ran a 'moderate' dictatorship, which had the Communist and APRA parties banned and their sympathisers prosecuted.[3] Eventually, pressure from the United States in particular forced him to organise free elections in 1939, which were won by the *Partido Civilista* (Civilist Party), and its candidate Manuel Prado Ugarteche became the next Peruvian president.

Ugarteche had few reasons to celebrate: almost immediately after his victory, reports of new clashes along the border with Ecuador surfaced, several of which resulted in casualties. In turn, this prompted the top commanders of the Peruvian military – most of whom were still loyal to Benavides – to start exerting pressure upon the new president. They faced him with a *de-facto* ultimatum, demanding he either take steps to guarantee the territorial sovereignty of the country or face a *coup d'etat*. Left with little choice, in December 1940 Ugarteche ordered the military to appoint an operations chief for the northern frontier, responsible for analysing the internal situation in Ecuador and studying the situation along the border, and then providing recommendations about boundary-related problems.

Before the Peruvian military could act according to Ugarteche's orders, through early January 1941 a series of reports was published in diverse newspapers and broadcast by radio stations in the Ecuadorean capital, announcing "clashes" in the north-eastern sector of the border. On 6 January 1941, a newspaper report even claimed that the Nangaritza province – in the border region of Zamora Chichipe – was occupied by Peruvian troops, while another announced an attack by Peruvian aviation against the Corral Viejo garrison, close to the border.

With the information provided by the intelligence services and following advice and plans issued by the High Command of the Army, on 11 January 1941 President Ugarteche issued a Supreme Decree, ordering the creation of the *Teatro de Operaciones del Norte* (TON, Northern Operations Theatre) and *Teatro de Operaciones Nor-Oriente* (TONO, North-Eastern Operations Theatre). Both of these

accused by the local opposition of having declared void the 1936 elections in order to deny victory to his enemies, thereby remaining

Tumbes, 1941. A pair of Caproni Ca.310 Tipo Perú bombers, rudimentarily camouflaged with branches, on the dispersal area of the airfield. (Amaru Tincopa Gallegos Collection)

A nice aerial shot of a Fairey Fox IV from *72 Escuadrilla de Información Terrestre*. (*Museo Aeronáutico* via José Barrera)

Crews from 72 EIT in front of one of the unit's Fairey Fox IVs shortly after arriving in Talara, where the unit was under the command of 1 GA. (Amaru Tincopa Gallegos Collection)

army groups were composed of ground, air and naval elements and were put under the command of Peruvian Army officers General Eloy G. Ureta (TON) and General Antonio Silva Santisteban (TONO). Immediately afterwards, the commanders of the TON and TONO were ordered to "implement a pacification operation" against southern and south-eastern territory in Ecuador.

The CAP, of course, was a key component of these forces and, in order to provide aerial units for TON and TONO, the *Ministerio de Marina y Aviation* assigned the 1 GA and 4 GA – led by Commanders Cesar Alvarez Guerra and Manuel Escalante P., and based at Chiclayo and Iquitos, respectively – to provide parts of their units to the TON and TONO. Precise details on the units in question are listed below.

I. – *Primer Grupo Aéreo*

This was the CAP's oldest operating unit outside the capital, based at Teniente Coronel Pedro Ruiz Gallo air base, located on the outskirts of the city of Chiclayo about 710km north of the capital Lima. This aerial wing was composed of the following elements:

(a) *XI Escuadrón de Bombardeo*

Considered to be the most modern and powerful unit within the CAP, this squadron was completely equipped with aircraft of Italian origin. It comprised the *11, 12* and *13 Escadrilles*, the first two each equipped with three Caproni Ca.310 Tipo Perú light bombers, while the last fielded six Caproni Ca.135 Tipo Perú medium bombers. This squadron also contained the most select Peruvian aviators and was organised as listed in Table 3.

Table 3: Pilots of *XI Escuadrón de Bombardeo*

Unit	Pilot
	Commanding Officer CAP Humberto Gal'Lino D.
11 Escadrille	Captain CAP Humberto Buenaño R.
	Lieutenant CAP Otto Gastelumendi M.
	Lieutenant CAP Jaime Cayo M.
	2nd Lieutenant Eduardo Montero R.
	2nd Lieutenant CAP Esteban Kisic Ch.
12 Escadrille	Captain Pedro Aguilar M.
	Lieutenant CAP Teodomiro Gabilondo U.
	Lieutenant CAP Marcial Burgos L.
	2nd Lieutenant CAP Teobaldo González C.
	2nd Lieutenant Jorge Calmell del Solar Z.
13 Escadrille	Captain Raúl Ravines B.
	Lieutenant Rafael León de la F.
	2nd Lieutenant Bernardino Valencia M.
	2nd Lieutenant Julio Suárez Cornejo
	2nd Lieutenant Enrique Mendiburu R.

(b) *XXI Escuadrón de Caza*

This squadron was composed of three *escadrilles* equipped with aircraft of Italian and American manufacture, in the form of North American NA-50 fighter-bombers and Caproni Ca.114 biplane fighters. The 1 AG also had a single Waco YKS tourism aircraft attached to serve as hack/VIP transport. The personnel of the *XXI Escuadrón de Caza* is listed in Table 4.

Table 4: Pilots of *XXI Escuadrón de Caza*

Unit	Pilot
	Commanding Officer Lieutenant CAP Antonio Alberti B.
41 Escadrille	Lieutenant CAP Fernando Paraud D.
	Lieutenant CAP Renán Elías O.
	Lieutenant CAP José Quiñones G.
	Lieutenant CAP Manuel Rivera L.A.
42 Escadrille	Captain CAP David Roca V.
	2nd Lieutenant CAP César Garcés
	2nd Lieutenant CAP José Winder A.
43 Escadrille	Lieutenant CAP César Bielich M.
	Lieutenant CAP Jorge Soldi L.B.
	2nd Lieutenant CAP Rolando Gervasi B.
	2nd Lieutenant CAP Alfonso Terán

II. – *Cuarto Grupo Aéreo*

The *Cuarto Grupo Aéreo* (4 GA, Fourth Air Group) was the aerial wing that operated in the Peruvian Amazonian territories. Its main base was Teniente Gustavo Cornejo seaplane station, located near the city of Iquitos, and it was composed of different combat and transport squadrons whose task was to provide defence, supplies and communication for the vast Peruvian Amazon region. The units of this group comprised the TONO aerial component.

(a) *LI Escuadrón de Aviación*

This was composed of two units: the *81 Escuadrilla de Combate* (81 EC, 81 Combat Squadron), equipped with three Curtiss model 37F Cyclone Falcons, and the *101 Escuadrilla de Transporte* (101 ET, 101 Transport Squadron), with two Grumman G-21 Goose, one Stinson-Faucett F.19, one Keystone K-55, one Hamilton H-45, one Stearman C-3R, a Waco YKS and a single Travelair B-6000S. All the aircraft assigned to these units were either flying boats or float-equipped airplanes. Pilots of the *LI Escuadrón de Aviación* are listed in Table 5.

Table 5: Pilots of *LI Escuadrón de Bombardeo*

Unit	Pilot
	Commanding Officer Commander Manuel Escalante
81 Escuadrilla de Combate	Captain Jorge Balarin de la Torre
	Lieutenant Carlos Benavides Dorich
	Lieutenant Jorge Morzan Arrarte
101 Escuadrilla de Transporte	Captain Carlos Moya Alvarado
	Lieutenant Jorge Cevallos Carbajal
	2nd Lieutenant Francisco Gabilondo U.

In the meantime, the *Ministerio de Marina y Aviación* (MMA, Marine and Aviation Ministry), with the objective of increasing the

Fighters from the XXI EC being readied for another day of operations from Tumbes forward airfield during the first days of July 1941. (Amaru Tincopa Gallegos Collection)

Two precariously camouflaged Ca.310s belonging to the *11 Escadrille*, XI EB, flank a Ca.111 transport from the 105 ET at Tumbes forward airfield on 16 July 1941. (Amaru Tincopa Gallegos Collection)

A pair of Ca.310 bombers, a single Waco YKS and a pair of Ca.111 transports parked between sorties at Tumbes forward airfield, which served as headquarters for the 1 GA. (Amaru Tincopa Gallegos Collection)

operational level of some of the aerial units assigned to the TON, ordered the reinforcement of the *XI Escuadron de Bombardeo* and *XXI Escuadron de Caza*, which received four Ca.310s and a similar number of Ca.114s respectively. These aircraft, which had been kept stored at Las Palmas as reserve, were flown to Chiclayo, where they were distributed between the different squadrons equipped with these types. With this measure, the MMA hoped to ensure that the units assigned to the TON could effectively carry out their assignments in spite of the low serviceability rates that plagued the CAP's Italian aircraft fleet.

The MMA also ordered the command of the *105 Escuadrilla de Transporte* (105 ET, 105 Transport Squadron), equipped with five Caproni Ca.111 bombers converted into transports, to deploy its unit to Chiclayo to provide supply and transport duties for the plethora of ground and air units deployed to the border as part of the TON. This unit, with its home base at Las Palmas airfield, was commanded by Captain Atilio Coli and was composed of officer pilots listed in Table 6.[4]

Table 6: Pilots of *105 Escuadrilla de Transporte*

Unit	Pilot
105 Escuadrilla de Transporte	Commanding Officer Captain Atilio Coli B.
	Captain Antonio Rojas Cadillo
	2nd Lieutenant Luis Benavides M.
	2nd Lieutenant Eduardo Wensjoe M.
	Lieutenant Jorge Morzan Arrarte

This unit's aircraft were later reinforced with the arrival of a pair of Curtiss BT-32 Condors and two Junkers Ju-52g3ms.[5]

In addition to the aforementioned squadrons, the MMA kept the following units under operational alert and ready to deploy to the operations theatres:

1. – *XXXI Escuadrón de Informacion y Ataque*

The *XXXI Escuadrón de Información y Ataque* (XXXI EIA, XXXI Information and Attack Squadron) was a tactical reconnaissance and attack unit with its home base at Las Palmas in Lima, equipped with nine Douglas 8A-3Ps, equally distributed among three squadrons, the 91st, 92nd and 93rd.[6] The officers assigned to this unit are listed in Table 7.

Table 7: Pilots of *XXXI Escuadrón de Informcion y Ataque*

Unit	Pilot
	Commanding Officer Lieutenant Commander Manuel García M.
91 Escadrille	Captain Enrique Ciriani Santa Rosa
	Lieutenant Jesús Melgar E.
	Lieutenant Enrique de Bernardi L.
92 Escadrille	Captain Enrique Bernales B.
	Lieutenant Enrique Escribens C.
	Lieutenant César Linch Cordero
93 Escadrille	Captain Salvador Noya Ferré
	Lieutenant Alberto Peña H.
	2nd Lieutenant Aníbal Maúrtua S.

One of the Caproni Ca.111 transport aircraft assigned to the 105 ET prepares to land on the runway of Teniente Coronel Pedro Ruiz Gallo air base in Chiclayo. The aircraft still sports the markings from its previous unit, the *11 Escadrille*, XI EB. (Amaru Tincopa Gallegos Collection)

Side view of the North American NA-50 serial XXI-41-3, factory number 50-951. This was the aircraft in which Lieutenant José Abelardo Quiñones Gonzales was killed during the attack on Ecuadorian positions in Quebrada Seca on 23 July 1941. (Amaru Tincopa Gallegos Collection)

Aerial view of NA-50 XXI-41-1, assigned to the commanding officer of the *41 Escadrille*, Commander Antonio Alberti. Note the diagonal bands on the fuselage and wings, identifying it as the unit leader's aircraft. (Amaru Tincopa Gallegos Collection)

Chiclayo, July 1941. Engine failures were a common occurrence for the Caproni Ca.135 Tipo Perú . This aircraft, identified with the serial XI-13-1, flown by Lieutenant León De la Fuente, suffered a fire in its right engine during a bombardment drill outside Chiclayo, forcing its pilot to perform an emergency landing. The aircraft was repaired and participated in the conflict. (Sergio de la Puente Collection)

An interesting picture showing the crews and ground personnel from XXI EC at Tumbes forward airfield on the morning of 22 July. Note the NA-50 loaded in the ground attack configuration, carrying four 15kg bombs and a pair of 50kg weapons in underwing racks. This is the last known picture of Lieutenant Quiñones (standing on the cockpit of his aircraft) before his death the next day. (IEHAP)

Ground crews perform a field engine change on a Caproni Ca.111 from the 105 ET at Talara airfield on 23 July 1941. (Sergio de la Puente Collection)

2. – *XXXII Escuadrón de Información Maritima*

This was a maritime reconnaissance unit with a home base at Alférez Carlos Huguet air base at Ancón Bay, about 40km north of Lima. This squadron was composed of the *82, 83* and *84 Escadrilles*, all equipped with seaplanes and flying boats. The *82 Escadrille*, with a trio of Curtiss model 37F Cyclone Falcons, was dedicated to the maritime reconnaissance, naval cooperation and light attack role, while the *83 Escadrille*, flying a similar number of Vought V-80P Corsair biplane seaplane fighters, was assigned to the maritime fighter role. The *84 Escadrille* was assigned to transport and liaison duties and flew an exotic mixture of aircraft, which included a pair of Grumman G-21 Goose flying boats, two Stinson-Faucett F-19 transport monoplanes (fitted with floats) and one each of the veteran O2U-1E Corsair and Stearman C-3R biplanes. Pilots assigned to the 82 EIM are listed in Table 8.

Table 8: Pilots of *82 Escuadrón de Información Maritima*	
Unit	Pilot
	Commanding Officer Captain Augusto Duarte C.
82 Escadrille	2nd Lieutenant Alberto López C.
	2nd Lieutenant Ernesto Fernández Lañas
	2nd Lieutenant José Heighes Pérez Albela[7]
Ground Echelon, Chief	2nd Lieutenant (Medical) Carlos Glave V.

Since this squadron's main role was cooperation with naval forces, the Peruvian *Marina de Guerra* designated a pair of officers as observers with the aim to ensure adequate coordination between surface and aviation units.

3. – *72 Escuadrón de Información Terrestre*

Based at Las Palmas, the *72 Escuadrón de Información Terrestre* (72 EIT, 72 Terrestrial Information Escadrille) was a tactical reconnaissance and army cooperation unit. It was equipped with five Fairey Fox IV, manned by pilots listed in Table 9.

Table 9: Pilots of *72 Escuadrón de Información Terrestre*	
Unit	Pilot
	Commanding Officer Captain Fernando Ordóñez de la Haza
pilots	Lieutenant Francisco García Romero
	Lieutenant Carlos Márquez G.
	2nd Lieutenant Francisco Cavero C.
	2nd Lieutenant Hernán Muñiz P.
	2nd Lieutenant Hartwing Holler W.
	2nd Lieutenant Dante Monge R.
	2nd Lieutenant Raúl Pinillos B.

These were the elements available to both the TON and TONO at the start of the hostilities. It is worth mentioning that these forces represented nearly 60 per cent of the total CAP strength at the time. The Peruvians also took care to deploy a number of liaison officers at forward air bases for CAP operations on the northern and north-eastern regions. These are listed in Table 10.

Table 10: Liaison Officers at Forward Air Bases
Pilot
Lieutenant Colonel Pedro Ruiz Gallo, home of the 1 GA, located in Chiclayo city
Lieutenant Gustavo Cornejo, Air Base, located in Iquitos city
Tumbes forward airfield[8]
Captain Guillermo Concha Iberico, connection airfield in Piura
Captain Victor Montes, connection airfield in Talara[9]
unknown officer at the Sullana connection airfield in Piura
unknown officer at the Cabo Pantoja forward air base in Loreto

A Grumman G-21 Goose of the *84 Escuadrilla*, XXXII EIM, on a refuelling stop at Tingo Maria airfield in the high Amazon region. These flying boats proved very useful for liaison with and supply of Peruvian TONO garrisons. (Humberto Currarino Collection)

Ground crews from *11 Escadrille*, XI EB, busy provisioning the 12.7mm Scotti machine guns fitted to this *Libeccio*. (Sergio de la Puente Collection)

General Eloy G. Ureta, head of the TON, descends from a Ca.310 *Libeccio* after completing a reconnaissance flight over the operations' front on 24 July 1941. (Sergio de la Puente Collection)

This rear view of the Ca.310 coded XIV-22-3, one of the machines from the recently disbanded XIV EB which was assigned to the XI EB in order to reinforce it, allows us to appreciate details of the defensive armament as well as its characteristic mixed construction fuselage. It was taken at Talara in late July 1941. (Sergio de la Puente Collection)

Ground personnel from XI EB unload 15kg and 50kg bombs from a truck under the watchful eye of an officer from the *11 Escadrille*. A local modification allowed the bomb rack fitted to the CAP *Libeccio* bombers to carry both Italian- and North American-made bombs. (IEHAP)

A trio of Ca.310 from *12 Escadrille* overflying a typical landscape found on the western Peru-Ecuador border as they head to attack objectives inside Ecuadorian territory on 24 July 1941. (Sergio de la Puente Collection)

3

THE ECUADOREAN MILITARY

In comparison to the Peruvian military of the late 1930s, the Ecuadorean military and Ecuadorean Army Aviation (hereafter AE) were diminutive. Indeed, the latter was a small service fielding hardly a fraction of the CAP's strength and capabilities.

Ground Forces

The Ecuadorean military traces its origins to the rebel forces of the independent state of Quito that fought against the Spanish royalist army of the Viceroy of Peru from 1809-22. Upon the dissolution of Gran Colombia in 1830, a majority of the Army's 2,000 officers and troops were Venezuelans (as was Ecuadorean first president, Juan José Flores), organised into three infantry battalions and one cavalry regiment. Indeed, even as of 1845, only four out of 14 general officers were Ecuadoreans, while non-natives comprised most of the officer corps and non-commissioned officers. This trend began to change in 1851, when General Urbina freed the black slaves and recruited many of them into the military.

After the Civil War of 1859-60, the Ecuadorean military was reformed, professionalised and depoliticised. Further improvements took place under military dictator General Ignacio de Veintemilla in the 1880s and 1890s, when French advisors were contracted to provide training on newly acquired armament. The first military educational facilities were established after the war with Colombia in 1900, and the country divided into four defence zones. By 1914, the Army had nine infantry battalions, three cavalry regiments, three artillery regiments and three engineering battalions: however, the decades-long build-up was discontinued and the military largely destroyed during the rebellion in the northern province of Esmeraldas, led by General Eloy Alfaro, in the period 1913-16.

Rebuilt by General Leonidas Plaza – who significantly improved cooperation between branches – the military was expanded to 15 infantry battalions by the mid-1920s. Under the influence of an Italian

military mission, this was reduced to 10 battalions, but each of these consisted of four rather than the earlier two or three rifle companies. By 1930, the ground force totalled about 5,500 officers and other ranks: however, continuous political unrest in the following years resulted in its massive weakening and disorganisation.

Ecuadorean Army Aviation

The aviation in Ecuador had its beginnings on 6 November 1912 when the first aircraft – a Farman with a 50hp engine belonging to the Chilean Eduardo Molina Lawin – arrived in the country. This aeroplane made several demonstration flights in the city of Guayaquil, taking off from the local Jockey Club. Ecuadorean Army Major Julio E. Jáuregui, the city's Military Chief, became the first Ecuadorean to fly by aircraft when he was invited to take part in one of those early flights.

In 1911, with the intention of supporting aerial activities in the country, the Guayas Car and Aviation Club organised a collection to prepare the first Ecuadorean pilot for training abroad. This resulted in the selection of Cosme Rennella Barbatto to be enrolled in the Chiribiri & C. Society Aviation School in Mirafiori, Turin, Italy, where he completed his training as a pilot on 28 August 1912. Subsequently, Rennella, always under the sponsorship of the aforementioned organisation, flew the first aircraft operated by the Ecuadorean Military Aviation: a Chiribri No.5 two-seater monoplane powered by a 50hp Gnome Rhone engine that arrived on 8 October 1913. This aircraft was christened *Patria No.1* and made its test flights, in front of an enthusiast crowd, from the local Jockey Club. Another precursor of aviation in Ecuador was Pedro Traversari Infante, an Army officer who had obtained his military aviator brevet in Chile on 16 August 1917. This officer carried out demonstration flights in Guayaquil aboard a Bleriot XI in June 1919 and June 1920.

However, the definitive impulse for the creation of military aviation

Among the few aircraft acquired by the Ecuadorean Military Aviation during the 1930s were at least one pair of Curtiss CW-14 Ospreys, a development from the Travelair 2000 series. (Dan Hagedorn Collection)

occurred through an enthusiastic journalist from Guayaquil named José Abel Castillo, who was the owner of *El Telégrafo* (*Telegraph*) newspaper and who from his own pocket acquired a Hanriot HD.1 biplane which he named *Telegrafo I*. This aircraft, piloted by Italian aviator Elia Antonio Liut, made its first flight in Guayaquil on 8 August 1920. Colonel Francisco Gomez de la Torre, Chief of the Military Zone of Guayaquil, after witnessing the flight, sent a telegram to Ecuadorean President Dr José Luis Tamayo as well as to the Army Chief of Staff, in which he stressed the enormous importance that aviation had and the need to support this new branch of the armed forces. Shortly afterwards, on 27 October 1920, a decree born from an executive initiative supported by the Congress was issued, authorising the establishment of the military aviation school in Quito, the capital, and another in Guayaquil, the second largest city of Ecuador. Then, on 27 December of the same year, a contract was signed with the French government for the provision, for a period of one year, of a French aeronautical mission that comprised pilot Marc Guitteny and mechanic Andre Jannin.

In the meantime, Elia Liut, who had been appointed as aviation instruction head by the Ecuadorean government, travelled to Europe, where he brought – with funds obtained through donations made by Ecuadorean society – aircraft for the newly established schools. These were a S.A.M.L.S.2, purchased in Italy by the Syrian colony of Guayaquil; an Ansaldo S.V.A.10, donated by the Italian colony; a Macchi M.18 hydrofoil, the most modern in its time, bought by the Chinese colony; an Aviatik B.I, bought in Italy by university students in Guayaquil, and a SALMSON 2A.2 biplane.

On 5 June 1921, the government issued a resolution creating the *Escuela de Aviación Militar* (Military Aviation School) and a few weeks later, on Sunday 12 July, the "El Condor" aerodrome and Aviation School was officially opened in Duran, in Guayas province, with Lieutenant Commander Juan Francisco Anda serving as its first director. Lack of funds, however, slowed the pace of training, and it was only on 2 June 1924 that the second aviation training course began at this school.

In October 1926, a group of seven Ecuadorean officers travelled to the city of Cameri in Italy, where they received instruction at the *Scuola di Aviazione Gabardini*, a process that proved to be most unfortunate as four of them were killed during the training process. The remaining three returned to Ecuador in November 1927. On 21 November 1927, the Department of Aviation was created as a branch of the Ministry of War, Navy and Aviation.

In another attempt to promote aviation in the country, on 28 February 1928, Captain Luis Mantilla successfully made a flight between the cities of Quito and Tulcán aboard a 120hp Gabardini Alpi biplane, christened "*NAPO*".

On 10 May 1929, the National Assembly authorised the construction of a new aerodrome in Guayaquil and, by the end of that year, it was decided to move the Military Aviation School at Duran to a new aerodrome in Latacunga. There, a number of new aircraft were received in late 1933, including a pair of Curtiss-Wright CW-14R Ospreys, which were pressed into service with the school. Operations at this airfield, however, became disrupted and came to a halt on 29 January 1934 when a fire destroyed the facilities, forcing the flight training school to move to Quito.

In 1935, Ecuadorean President elect Dr José María Velasco Ibarra firmly proposed to attend to and solve the problems of the *Aviación Militar Ecuatoriana* (AME, Ecuadorean Military Aviation) and, as a token of his will, signed a contract for the procurement of eight Curtiss-Wright CW-16E trainers and ordered the recruitment of experienced flight instructors. The president also ordered the reconditioning of the "Simón Bolívar" airfield in Guayaquil, which included the construction of facilities for maintenance hangars, administrative buildings and barracks. By Executive Decree No.692, of 3 July 1935, the Military Aviation School was created in the city of Guayaquil, at "Simón Bolívar" Airport, with Major Luis A. Mantilla appointed as its director.

Continuing with the procurement efforts for new aircraft, the Ecuadorean government signed a contract with the Curtiss Aviation and Motor Co. on 13 August 1935 for the acquisition of six Curtiss CW-19R aircraft, known as "Curtiss Trainers", for a total of $42,900. These aircraft were delivered in September 1936 and received the serials 51-56. Two months after issuing the order, the Ecuadorean government signed a contract with American pilot James H. Gray to become technical instructor at the Military Aviation School. Another important step taken in the professionalisation of the Ecuadorean

Undoubtedly the most capable aircraft in the AME inventory were three Curtiss CW-19Rs, survivors of six aircraft acquired in 1936. These metallic monoplanes were used almost exclusively for reconnaissance and liaison work. (Dan Hagedorn Collection)

In 1936, the AME received eight of the 10 Curtiss CW-16Es ever manufactured. Essentially a three-seat version of the CW-12 series, these were powered with the 125hp Kinner B-5 engine. One of these aircraft was forced to land in Tumbes in 1937 after violating Peruvian airspace. After dealing with the incident through the chancelleries, the aircraft and crew were able to return to Ecuador. (Amaru Tincopa Gallegos Collection)

Military Aviation was the creation, on 1 January 1936, of the Aviation Inspectorate, subordinated to the War and Navy Ministry.

The need to have more modern airplanes to equip its precarious military aviation led the Ecuadorean government to look in different countries for an economic and effective solution to their requirements. An approach to the Italian government at the beginning of 1937 led to a proposal from the *Industrie Meccaniche Aeronautiche Meridionali* (IMAM) for the sale of a batch of IMAM Ro.37Bis observation and light attack biplanes, with the price including both the local training of crews for these aircraft as well as the commitment to receive Ecuadorean Military Aviation cadets into Italian aviation schools. The payment terms presented to Ecuador by the *Consorzio Italiano della Esportazioni Aeronautiche* – the fascist government aircraft and engines export sales bureau – were acceptable to the government of President Federico Páez Chiriboga, who issued an order for nine aircraft in February of that year.

The aircraft ordered by Ecuador began to arrive at the beginning of April 1937, while the Italian military mission, which was contracted through the same sale agreement, arrived in May that year. The task of this mission, led by Major Amedeo Micciani and composed of Colonel Giacomo Negroni, Lieutenant Colonel Alessandro Brutini, Captain Higilio Perotti and Lieutenants Aurelio Laino and Pietro Palmerino, was to train crews in the proper handling of their aircraft as well as in the tactics of modern aerial warfare in accordance with the latest doctrines developed and employed by the Italian *Regia Aeronautica*.

Upon its arrival, the Italian military mission proceeded to train the Ecuadorean pilots in their new mounts without major setbacks, as the large biplanes were nimble aircraft that had no major vices and handled well. However, a problem arose within a few weeks of their introduction as it became evident that the same good qualities present in the design were completely absent in the quality control of the materiel and components. The aircraft's Piaggio engines – especially their carburettors – proved unreliable and were prone to failure, as were other critical parts of the aircraft such as its landing gear, which needed reinforcement as they were prone to collapse at the slightest carelessness of some cadet. Despite these problems, the crews completed their training cycle and the 16th Squadron was soon declared operational.

The Ro.37 had an unfortunate service record with the Ecuadorean Military Aviation. On 2 November 1938, a heterogeneous *escadrille* composed of seven aircraft of different types was gathered at "El Condor" airfield at Eloy Alfaro, near Guayaquil, to take part in ceremonies to be held in the city of Cuenca during that month. Bad weather, however, caused the dispersion of the group and only a few aircraft were able to reach Cuenca, with others forced to head back to Guayaquil. Among the latter was Ro.37Bis serial 16-4 flown by Captain Carlos Cabezas, also carrying Captain Gonzalo Gallo, which disappeared *en route* to Guayaquil, and – after four days of intense search – was found completely destroyed near "*Los Soldados*" field in El Cañar province. Poor weather and lack of training were the alleged causes of this accident.

Another IMAM was lost, this time fortunately without casualties, in April 1939 when Ro.37Bis serial 16-1 was written-off after a mechanical failure. Shortly after, another incident involving a Ro.37Bis left a pilot injured when his aircraft, serial 16-3, crashed during a training flight near Quito. The mounting number of accidents led the Ecuadorean government to place an order for an additional Ro.37 as replacement in the summer of 1939 to maintain the aerial operations of the 16 EOB. By that time, however, some AM officers had apparently become disaffected with the aircraft, as addressed by a note from the US Naval attaché in Guayaquil who reported that at least two officers requested to be discharged from active duty before continuing flying the type.

On 10 November 1939, a new tragedy hit the Ecuadorean Military Aviation. Lieutenant Gabriel Gangotena – considered the best acrobatic pilot in the country – took off from Mariscal Sucre airfield in Quito aboard the Ro.37 serial 16-6, with Private Miguel Angel Arias as passenger, for a test flight. Shortly after take-off, however, at a height of 400 metres, an engine failure developed and it caught fire a few moments after. Lieutenant Gangotena tried to return to the airfield to save the aircraft but was unable to clear a line of trees located in front of the runway, crashing his aircraft and being killed along with his passenger. There was even more grief for Ecuadorean flyers, for on 29 November another IMAM (serial number 16-7) plunged to earth after taking off from Mariscal Sucre due to mechanical failure, killing both occupants.

To identify the causes and responsibility behind the latest incidents that affected the Ro.37 fleet, an investigation was ordered by Ecuadorean Military Aviation authorities, with official report no.209/ris directed to the Aviation Inspector, Colonel Luis A. Rodríguez. The report stated that the Piaggio engines lacked spare parts and had been irresponsibly operated for more than the 175 hours recommended by the factory. This critical situation was a consequence of the lack of funds available to the military aviation, which in turn was caused by the political instability engulfing the Ecuadorean government during that period. As a result, the engines of the IMAMs could not be properly checked nor the spare parts required obtained, a situation that led to low availability and, eventually, accidents. Politicians blamed the Italian mission labour as the chief culprit for the incidents, accusing it of irresponsible behaviour "by operating the aircraft against the regulations and therefore acting against the preservation of the flight material". This was the excuse behind the decision not to renew the Italian mission contract and, as a consequence, the Italians were sent back home at the end of 1939.

The situation with the Ro.37 fleet had become unsustainable by 1940, and by 21 December only two out of the five remaining aircraft still appeared in the Ecuadorean Military Aviation order of battle, although marked as non-operational. As border clashes increased and the bilateral relationship between Ecuador and Peru worsened, an attempt was made to bring these two airframes back into airworthy condition with the dedicated ground personnel at Simon Bolívar AB performing urgent maintenance and repairs. These efforts, however, proved fruitless, as stated in report no.516H dated 17 July 1941, issued by the aviation inspector, Major Jorge Páez M., who ordered the aircraft to be indefinitely withdrawn from service due to the impossibility of returning them to operative conditions.

The Ecuadorean Military Aviation thus arrived at the events of 5 July with only a few training and liaison aircraft available to counter the might of a well-prepared CAP. At the time hostilities broke out, the AE operated just a handful of aircraft, all of limited combat value, which included the following:

- Five Curtiss-Wright CW-19R Sparrows (three airworthy)[1]
- Five IMAM Ro.37Bis (none operational)
- Two Curtiss CW-14R Ospreys[2]
- Three Curtiss CW-16E Trainers[3]
- Two Ju-52g/3ms from SEDTA[4]
- A single Douglas DC-2 (formerly PANAGRA)[5]

From these, only the CW-19R Sparrow monoplanes could be considered as valuable assets from a military point of view, being the sole aircraft in the Ecuadorean strength – still in an airworthy condition – that could be fitted with bombs and machine guns.[6] The three available Sparrows, with serial numbers 50, 51 and 53, were the main participants in the few missions launched by the AE over the frontier during the conflict.[7] The air bases and airfields used by the Ecuadorean Army Aviation as of July 1941 are listed in Table 11.

Table 11: Ecuadorean Air Bases and Airfields, June 1941	
Base	**Geographic Area**
Simón Bolívar Airport	Guayaquil
Mariscal Sucre Airport	Quito
Cotopaxi Airport	Latacunga
Chimborazo Airport	Riobamba
Mariscal La Mar airfield	Cuenca
Santa Rosa airfield	
Loja airfield	
Mecará airfield	
Célica airfield	
Bellavista airfield	
Salinas airfield	

As of 5 July, the AE included two commanding officers, 36 pilot-officers, four service officers, 219 non-commissioned officers and 506 air reserve members (all unarmed). Of all of these men, only the following were available to operate the small fleet of readily available aircraft:

- Major Leónidas Hidalgo
- Captain Bayardo Tobar
- Captain Gonzalo García
- Lieutenant Bolívar Pico
- Lieutenant Teodoro Carrión
- Lieutenant Rafael Ramos
- Lieutenant Alfredo Arteaga
- 2nd Lieutenant Víctor Suárez Haz
- 2nd Lieutenant Luis Arias Guerra

The *Lufthansa* incident

During November 1940, the German air navigation company *Deutsche Lufthansa*, through its offices in the city of Lima, requested the Commercial and Civil Aviation Directorate of Peru for authorisation for one of its Junkers Ju-52s, the *Aconcagua*, to be temporarily transferred to Ecuador to replace that country's Junkers Ju-52 HC-SAC Guayas, an airplane that until a few months ago had been flown by the Ecuadorean Society of Air Transportation (SEDTA). However, given the permit, the company did not take care to completely erase the Peruvian registration that was displayed under the wings and only proceeded to paint the tail with the Ecuadorean flag.

It was with these characteristics that, on 3 January 1941, the aircraft made a flight between Guayaquil and the province of Loja, during which it flew over Peruvian territory in the Zarumilla area, prompting the Peruvian Air Force to dispatch two NA-50 fighters, which escorted the Junkers all the way to Machala, inside Ecuadorean territory. This event caused great commotion and discomfort in both countries. The Peruvians first reaction to the incident was the imposition of a fine against *Deutsche Lufthansa* operations for "allowing the overflight of an aircraft using Peruvian registration and Ecuadorean markings". A short time later, via a Supreme Resolution of 20 March 1941, the Peruvian government decided to punish the Germans' operations by reducing the concession granted to the local branch of *Deutsche Lufthansa* from an original three-year permit to only 90 days after publication of the document. It is worth mentioning that during this period, the company's flights were only allowed to operate with a CAP officer aboard.

In the meantime, in Ecuador things got even more serious as the Ecuadorean media duly published a statement from the SEDTA general

A clear shot of Ju-52 registered OA-HHA seen at Limatambo international airport at the beginning of 1939. This particular aircraft was confiscated by the Peruvian government in April 1941 and pressed into service with the CAP as a transport with civilian registry OB-HHA . (Amaru Tincopa Gallegos Collection)

An Italian military mission arrived in Ecuador in 1937 with the objective of reorganising its military forces. A number of pilot officers from the *Regia Aeronautica* provided training and advice to the Ecuadorean Military Aviation. Lieutenant Casarosa was one of these pilots, here seen with a pair of Ecuadorean aviators in front of a CW.19. (Roberto Gentili Collection)

Another picture of Lieutenant Casarosa with his pupils, taken at Simon Bolívar airfield in the city of Guayaquil. (Roberto Gentili Collection)

Probably all the Ecuadorean military pilots of the late 1930s portrayed in a single picture:
Lieutenant Casarosa and his students in 1937. (Roberto Gentili Collection)

manager that stated that "Peruvian warplanes entered Ecuadorean territory and intercepted an aircraft of its company." Needless to say, this created a huge scandal in the Ecuadorean government, with its chancellery issuing a note of protest against the Peruvian government.

On 5 July, the century-old boundary dispute escalated from skirmishes to an armed conflict, with reports of small-scale operations conducted across several scattered points over the 1,000-mile frontier reaching the capitals of both countries. Almost at once, on 9 July,

representatives of Brazil, Argentina and the United States started diplomatic efforts seeking troop withdrawals and the resumption of peaceful negotiations. The Peruvian government, however, having prepared its forces for several years in anticipation to such a scenario, decided to follow the advice of the military leadership and to end the dispute, once and for all, by way of force, ordering its forces in the TON and TONO to act in accordance with their plans.

4

PERUVIAN COMBAT OPERATIONS, JULY 1941

After finding out about the events in the north, the TON Command put in effect a number of directives for the execution of its defensive dispositions. In the case of the aviation, these included the immediate mobilisation of combat units and their deployment to the area of operations. With all the three wars fought by Ecuador and Peru being surrounded by an incredible number of myths, rumours and pure guesswork, and emotions running high whenever these are discussed, the lines between facts and fantasies have become heavily blurred over time. Therefore, instead of a typical – yet certainly controversial – narrative, the best way to cover the air war of 1941 is in the form of transcriptions of the official documentation, largely memorandums and orders registered in the (Peruvian) Air Force General Orders for the Year 1941.

5 July 1941

XXI EC – Three out of the five NA-50 available to the *41 Escadrille* were deployed to Talara, where they remained on alert.[1]

XI EB – The *11* and *12 Escadrilles* remained at Chiclayo on alert while repairs were completed on some of their aircraft. Meanwhile, a pair of Ca.135 bombers from *13 Escadrille* were sent to Piura and Tumbes to carry supplies.

105 ET – A total of three supply missions were flown between Tumbes, Chiclayo and the different airfields on the TON.

6 July

XXI EC – By order of Commander Cesar Alvarez Guerra, head of the 1 GA, the trio of NA-50s at Talara were redeployed to Tumbes during the early morning. These were within hours joined by their commanding officer, Lieutenant Commander Antonio Alberti, who arrived from Chiclayo. This order had the objective of providing air cover for the

city of Tumbes, as well as to the Army and Navy elements stationed nearby. At 1450 hours, a section of three aircraft armed with 50kg demolition bombs took off from Tumbes and headed to the border vigilance posts of Aguas Verdes, el Porvenir and La Palma in order to provide close support for EP forces that were under harassment by Ecuadorean troops. Meanwhile, the *42 Escadrille* received the order to deploy from Chiclayo to Talara in order to cover the gap caused by the departure of the *41 Escadrille*, remaining on alert once they arrived.

XI EB – This unit remained on alert at its base in Chichlayo.

105 ET – Ca.111 serial 105-2 flew supplies from Chiclayo to Talara, as a precaution against the staff increase in these premises. Meanwhile, Ca.111 105-3, on a mission in Tumbes, returned to Talara to transport supplies required by the operations of the *41 Escadrille* and returned to Tumbes in the afternoon.

7 July

XI EB – The *12 Escadrille* arrived at Talara with part of its complement (three aircraft), while two machines remained at Chiclayo undergoing maintenance. Meanwhile, the *11 Escadrille* remained on alert at that location, while two machines from the *13 Escadrille*, Ca.135 XI-13-1 and XI-13-2, were dispatched from Chiclayo to Talara carrying supplies and materiel required to support the operations of the *12* and *42 Escadrilles*.

XXI EC – In Tumbes, the *41 Escadrille* was tasked to perform a reconnaissance over the battlefront and to attack Ecuadorean forces located on the northern bank of the Zarumilla River. After completing the first sortie, and while the aircraft were still being rearmed for the next mission, an urgent order from TON command arrived, requesting the immediate interception of enemy planes spotted over the border town of Aguas Verdes, thus changing the mission priorities from close

MEMORANDUM Nº 10

P. C. TUMBES 31 DE JULIO 1941

AL   :   Comandante de la 105 Escuadrilla de Transporte y S. O.
                       de Aviación de 1ra. Antonio Brandariz.

1.   Información:

  a)   A las 11:45 hrs., un Piquete de Aviación, ha desembarcado en
       el campo de Santa Rosa, apoderándose de él sin mayor resis-
       tencia.

  b)   Se sabe por nuestro reconocimiento, que no hay casi actividad
       enemiga en los pueblos de Machala y Puerto Bolívar.

  c)   Un Piquete de Aviación a las 15:00 hrs., desembarcará en el cam-
       po a proximidad de Puerto Bolívar, con la misión de progresar
       hacia el puerto y tomar enlace con los Paracaidistas que
       Ud., comanda.

2.   El Comando de la 105 Escuadrilla de Transporte, dispondrá que su
     Unidad se encuentre lista para salir a una hora que se dará verbal-
     mente, transportando a los Paracaidistas cuya misión es lanzarse a la
     vertical de Puerto Bolívar, con el fin de apoderarse de dicho Puerto y
     mantenerse con todos sus medios a su alcance, estableciendo enlace
     previo con el Piquete que progresa del campo de aterrizaje a proxi-
     midad de Puerto Bolívar.

El Comando del Agrpto. Aéreo del Norte
Comandante C.A.P.
CESAR ALVAREZ GUERRA

Distrib.:   105 Esc.
            E.M.G.A.
            Archivo.

A copy of one of the documents used to prepare this chapter. (FAP Archive)

support to interception. However, despite the fast reaction of the unit and the almost immediate arrival of the fighters over Aguas Verdes, no trace of the alleged intruders was found. The flight then continued *en route* to complete its secondary mission: to attack Ecuadorean positions near the town of Chacras. During their return to base in Tumbes, the flight leader, Lieutenant Commander Antonio Alberti, ordered his men to head over the sea in order to drop their unused bombs to reduce the risk of an accidental explosion during landing. After all aircraft had released their ordnance, Alberti noticed that the aircraft XXI-41-2 flown by Lieutenant Renán Elías Olivera still had a bomb hanging from its rack, so the pilot was ordered to perform an emergency procedure in order to release the bombs.[2] Unfortunately, instead of performing a shallow dive and pull up, Lieutenant Elías waved his wings, trying to force the departure of the bomb, triggering the fuse with the movement and causing it to explode and destroy the aircraft, which burst into flames and fell into the sea with its unfortunate pilot. After overflying the impact area for some minutes looking for a trace of the ill-fated aviator, the remaining members of the patrol notified the headquarters about the incident and a Caproni Ca.111, serial 105-1, was dispatched to the area on a search mission, which proved unsuccessful.

In the meantime, in Talara, the *42 Escadrille* finished its relocation

with two additional Caproni Ca.114s flying in following the 1 GA command orders.

72 EIT – As a consequence of the urgent need to have a proper reconnaissance and Army cooperation, the Army HQ issued an official request to the Ministry of Marine and Aviation (MMA) for the deployment of the *72 Escadrille* Terrestrial Information (EIT) to the TON. Accordingly, and by MMA resolution issued that day, the unit became part of the organic elements of the TON and began its deployment to the conflict zone.

105 ET – Caproni 105-2 and 105-3 ferried from Chiclayo base to Talara the staff and materiel required for normal operations of the *12* and *42 Escadrilles*.

8 July
XI EB – *11* and *12 Escadrilles* registered no flying activity. In the meantime, two units of the *13 Escadrille* kept carrying supply sorties between Chiclayo and Talara and Tumbes airfields.

XXI EC – A four-aircraft formation took off from Tumbes to perform an interception against an Ecuadorean aircraft sighted over the Ecuadorean border posts at Chacras and Huaquillas, without results.

72 EIT – Prepared the staff and materiel before their displacement to TON.

A photograph showing the "facilities" available for crews at Tumbes forward airfield. Some details of the nose section of a Caproni Ca.114 fighter from *43 Escadrille* are also visible. (IEHAP)

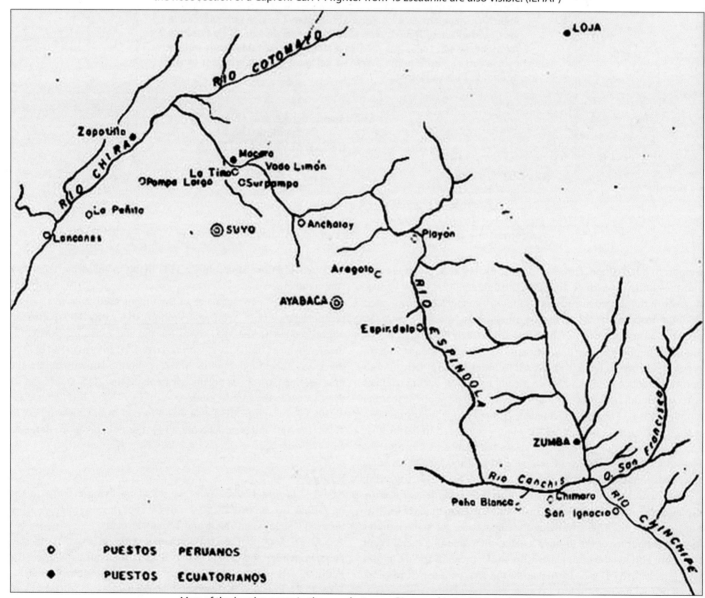

Map of the border posts in the area between Piura and Loja. (FAP Archive)

In an attempt to counter the rearming of the Peruvian aviation, Ecuador ordered nine IMAM Ro.37Bis observation and light attack aircraft in February 1937. Poor logistics, financial support and a series of unfortunate accidents meant that by the time of the conflict, only five remained on the strength, with none operational. (Artwork by Luca Canossa)

The Curtiss-Wright CW-19 was a civil utility aircraft designed by the Curtiss-Wright Co. It was built in small quantities in a number of variants. In 1936, Ecuador ordered six CW-19Rs, a light bombing variant armed with two .30 calibre machine guns (one fixed and one in a flexible mount in the rear cockpit) and two A-3 bomb racks. (Artwork by Luca Canossa)

The Junkers Ju-52 "Aconcagua", formerly operated by the Lufthansa subsidiary in Peru before being transferred to the Ecuadorean Society of Air Transportation (SEDTA), was responsible for a major diplomatic crisis when it flew, while still wearing its former Peruvian registration and national colours, over Ecuadorean territory in early 1941. (Artwork by Luca Canossa)

The Curtiss-Wright CW-16E was a high-performance trainer built by the Curtis Wright Corporation during the early 1930s. Ecuador purchased six CW-16Es, a model fitted with a Wright J-6 engine, in 1935 as part of government efforts to modernise its military aviation. (Artwork by Luca Canossa)

A Caproni Ca.310 *Libeccio* light bomber from the *12 Escuadrilla, XI Escuadrón de Bombardeo*, during the 1941 campaign. A total of 16 aircraft were ordered by the CAP in 1938 and suffered a high attrition rate, the highest of the period, with not less than four aircraft lost in accidents by December 1940. The *Libeccios* saw first-line service with the CAP until December 1943, when they were allocated to training duties. Like most of the CAP fleet, they were painted in silver dope overall, but many had their engine cowlings painted in vivid colours, for easier recognition. Inset is shown detail of an example from the XXI Escuadrón. (Artwork by Luca Canossa)

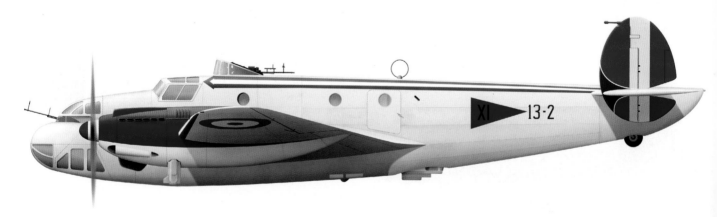

The Caproni Ca.135 bomber serial XI-13-2 flown by Captain Raul Ravines on 10 July 1941. This aircraft suffered an engine malfunction while returning from a reconnaissance mission over Machala and crash landed 50km east of Piura. (Artwork by Luca Canossa)

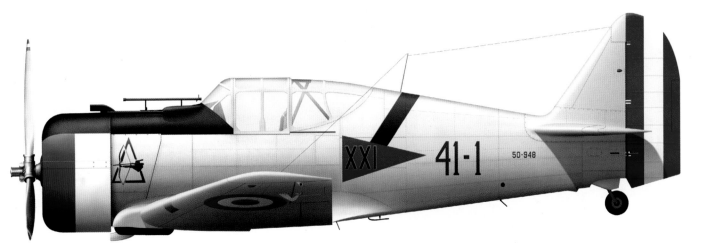

Seven North American NA-50 fighter bombers were purchased in late 1938 to equip the newly formed *XXI Escuadrón de Caza*. The NA-50 was a development of the NA-16 trainer fitted with a more powerful engine and retractable landing gear. It carried a pair of .30 calibre machine guns as well as underwing racks for light bombs. (Artwork by Luca Canossa)

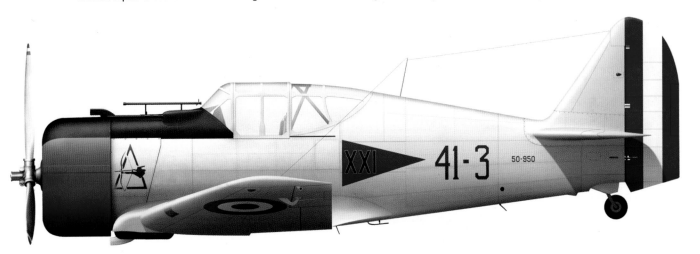

The North American NA-50 serial XXI-41-3 flown by Lieutenant José Quiñones during the attack against Ecuadorian positions in the Quebrada Seca-Carcabón area on 23 July 1941. All the NA-50s wore a bare metal finish and coloured cowlings for identification purposes. (Artwork by Luca Canossa)

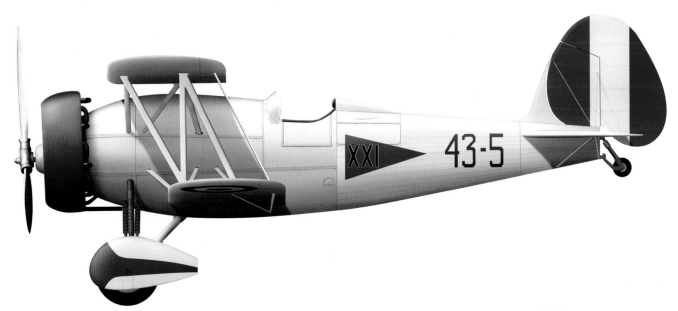

Peru purchased a dozen Caproni Ca.114 fighters in 1934 – contenders with the famous Fiat Cr.32 during the 1932 *Regio Aeronáutica's* new fighter programme. Twelve of these nimble fighters were acquired by the CAP and assigned to the *II Escuadrón de Caza*, based at Chichlayo. By 1941, the unit was reformed as the *XXI Escuadrón de Caza*. XXI-43-5 was a fighter assigned to the *43 Escuadrilla* during its deployment to Tumbes in late July 1941, remaining in service until that unit's disbandment in 1942. (Artwork by Luca Canossa)

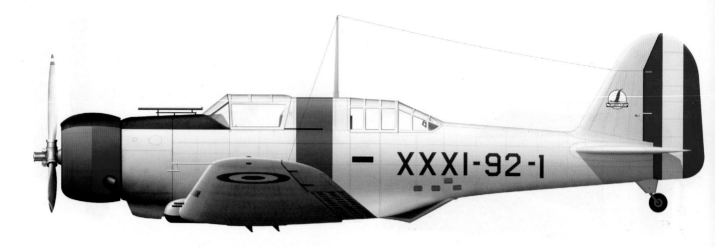

Influenced by the development of air warfare in the skies over Spain in the 1930s, the CAP high command saw the importance of integrating assault aircraft into its doctrine. As a consequence, 10 Douglas 8A-3Ps, a development of the Northrop A-17A attack aircraft series designed for export customers, were ordered in late 1938. The aircraft was powered by a more powerful Wright Cyclone engine and could carry 600kg of bombs. (Artwork by Luca Canossa)

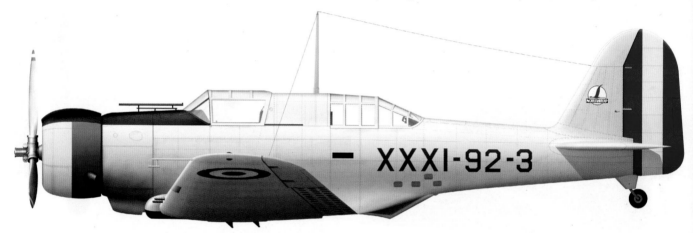

The Douglas 8A-3P assigned to the *92 Escuadrilla, XXXI Escuadrón de Información y Ataque* at Talara in late July 1941. The Douglas' from this unit replaced the NA-50s from XXI EC in attack and close-support duties in support of the Peruvian Army advance between 26 July and 10 August. Like the NA-50s, they were left in bare metal overall, but had their engine cowlings painted in different colours for easier identification. (Artwork by Luca Canossa)

The Peruvian Air Corps ordered ten Curtiss model 37F observation and light attack biplanes in 1934. This model, fitted with a Wright R-1820F Cyclone radial engine, was known as the "Cyclone" or "Export" Falcon and had a long operational life with Peruvian military aviation, being much appreciated by their crews thanks to its ease of maintenance and sturdiness. XXXII-82-3 was a "Cyclone Falcon" assigned to the command of the XXXII Escuadrón de Información Marítima and was deployed to Puerto Pizarro forward seaplane base during the conflict. (Artwork by Luca Canossa)

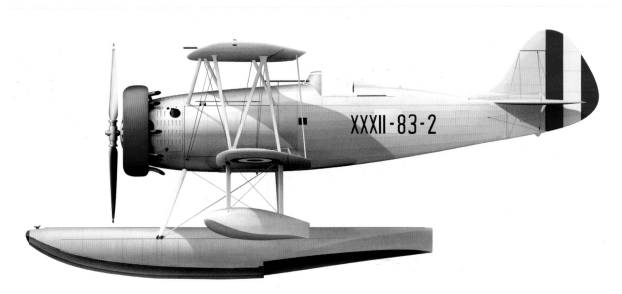

The V-80P was the most powerful and heavily armed of the Corsair biplane series. Fitted with a 750hp P&W Hornet engine, it was armed with four .30 calibre machine guns and could carry up to 200kg of bombs in underwing racks. These aircraft were delivered in 1933 and had a long life with Peruvian military aviation, the last being withdrawn from service in the mid-1950s. (Artwork by Luca Canossa)

In 1933, Peru ordered six Fairey Fox IVs, a combat-capable development of the Fox II equipped with a Kestrel IIS engine and floats. While these were delivered too late to take part in the Putumayo conflict, they eventually saw service in the maritime reconnaissance role with the *71 Escuadrilla de Información Marítima* (Maritime Information Escadrille) until December 1940, when this unit was disbanded and its aircraft pressed into service with the recently activated 72 EIT. (Artwork by Luca Canossa)

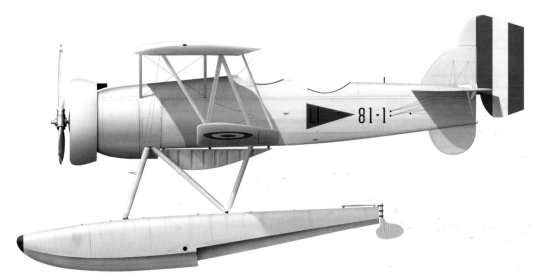

The Curtiss Cyclone Falcon serial LI-81-1 flown by Captain Balarin on an armed reconnaissance sortie over the Pastaza-Puesto Puyas axis. As usual, it was painted in silver dope overall and had a large tri-colour applied down the rudder. The Curtiss' from LI EA provided invaluable support to Peruvian Army ground forces in the TONO. (Artwork by Luca Canossa)

The CAP operated a couple Travelair B-6000 monoplanes in 1932-33. These were fitted with floats and assigned to transport duties in the Amazon. The LI EA operated the sole survivor of these monoplanes as part of the *101 Escuadrilla de Transporte*. (Artwork by Luca Canossa)

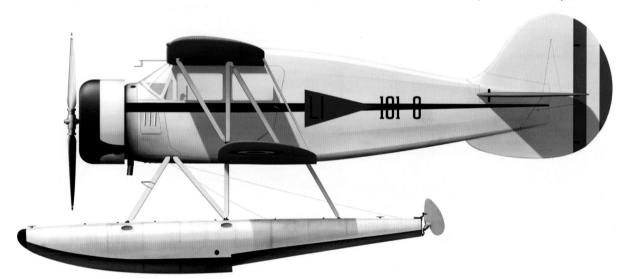

One of the most exotic types flown during the conflict was a single Waco YKS tourism biplane purchased in late 1939 and assigned to the *101 Escuadrilla de Transporte*. (Artwork by Luca Canossa)

The CAP ordered four Grumman G-21 Goose amphibious aircraft in 1938 to serve as liaison and transport aircraft in the vast Amazon territories. These sturdy and reliable aircraft remained in Peruvian military aviation service until the late 1940s. All were painted in silver dope overall, but had large parts of the forward and bottom fuselage (as well as engine nacelles) painted in black, a cheat-line painted in blue, and wore the usual national colours applied on the rudder. (Artwork by Luca Canossa)

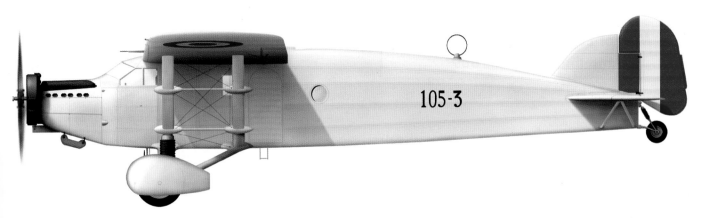

Caproni Ca.111 serial 105-3 was one of the survivors of the 12 Caproni Ca.111 bombers purchased in 1934. Originally fitted with floats and powered by Isotta Fraschini 750R engines, they were overhauled and fitted with the slightly more powerful – but more reliable - I.F. XI RC.40 Asso 940hp engine in 1938. With the arrival of the Caproni Ca.135 and Ca.310, the Ca.111 was relegated to transport duties. (Artwork by Luca Canossa)

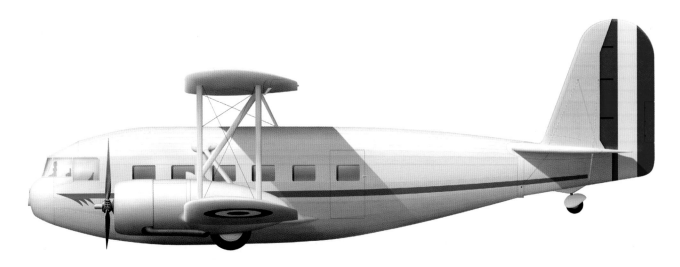

In 1935, four Curtiss BT-32 bombers *en-route* to Bolivia were interned by Peruvian authorities following the embargo on arm sales imposed upon that country by the League of Nations. After brief service as passenger aircraft in Peru, two surviving airframes were pressed into service with the CAP as transport aircraft. After an overhaul at the Caproni works in Lima, the Condors were pressed into service with the *105 Escuadrilla de Transporte*, still wearing their original livery of silver dope. (Artwork by Luca Canossa)

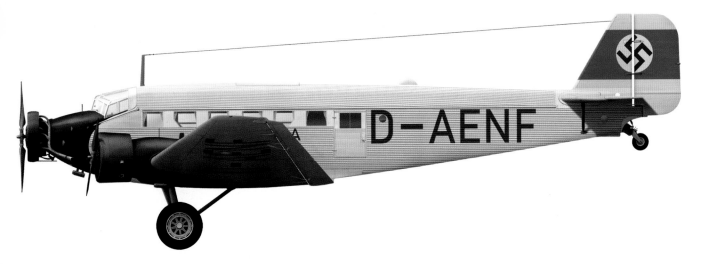

The *Deutsche Lufthansa* Peru branch operated in Peru between 24 May 1938 and 31 March 1941, when the Peruvian government withdrew its operation permit. The next day the Peruvians seized *Lufthansa*'s two Junkers Ju-52s and pressed them into service with the CAP. These aircraft were OA-HHC-304 (construction number 5272), christened *Huandoy*, and OA-HHA-294 (5283), named *Huascarán*.

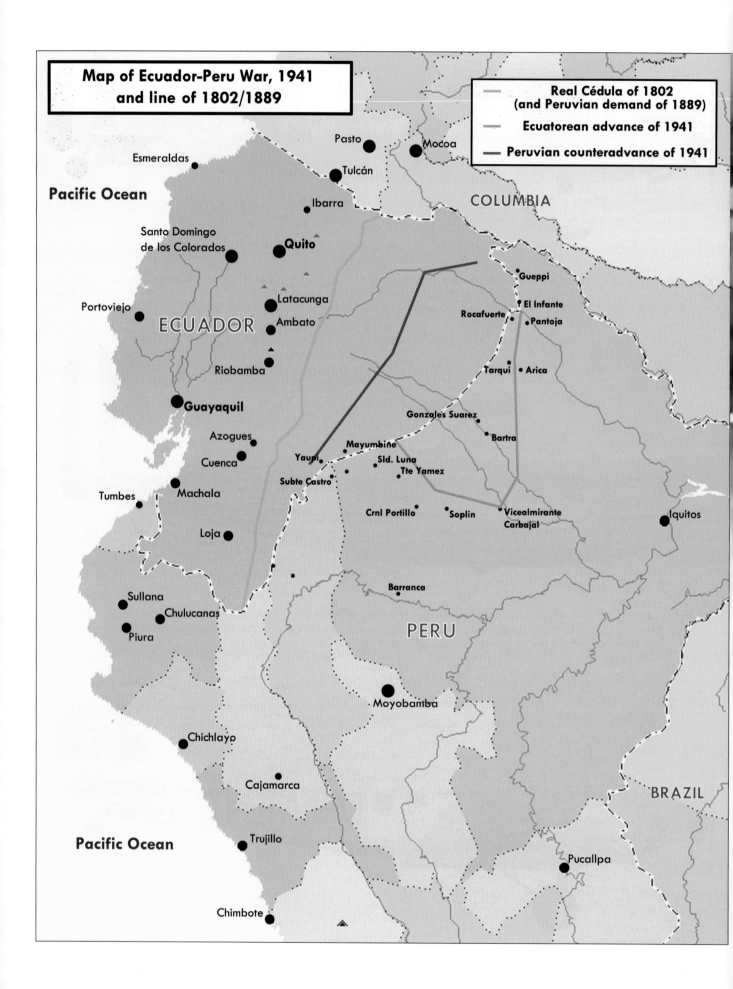

Map of Ecuador-Peru War, 1941 and line of 1802/1889

Real Cédula of 1802 (and Peruvian demand of 1889)
Ecuatorean advance of 1941
Peruvian counteradvance of 1941

Pasto
Mocoa
Tulcán

COLUMBIA

Esmeraldas

Pacific Ocean

Ibarra

Santo Domingo de los Colorados

Quito

Gueppi
El Infante
Rocafuerte
Pantoja

Portoviejo

Latacunga
Ambato

ECUADOR

Tarqui
Arica

Riobamba

Gonzales Suarez
Bartra

Guayaquil

Mayumbine
Yaupi
Sld. Luna
Tte Yamez
Subte Castro

Azogues

Cuenca

Tumbes
Machala

Crnl Portillo
Soplin
Vicealmirante
Carbajal

Iquitos

Loja

Barranca

Sullana
Chulucanas
Piura

PERU

Moyobamba

Chichlayo

Cajamarca

Trujillo

BRAZIL

Pacific Ocean

Pucallpa

Chimbote

105 ET – continued to ferry supplies for the CAP units stationed in Talara and Tumbes.

9 July

The units under the command of 1 GA registered no aerial operations.

72 EIT – The unit left Las Palmas air base at 0900 hours and arrived at Talara advanced sub-base that afternoon.

10 July

XI EB – *13 Escadrille* sent a Ca.135, flown by Captain Raul Ravines with serial XI-13-2, on a reconnaissance mission to Machala.[3] However, during its way back to Chiclayo and while approximately 50km east of Piura, the starboard engine overheated and stopped, forcing the pilot to perform a forced landing in a desolated area. Due to extensive damage to the underside of the aircraft and the impossibility of recovery, it was decided to abandon it *in situ* after all reusable equipment was recovered.

XXI EC – The command of 1 GA decided to transfer the *42 Escadrille* from Talara to Tumbes in lieu of the *41 Escadrille* to relieve this unit, whose members were showing symptoms of fatigue from the constant activity sustained since the beginning of the campaign. After arrival, the *42 Escadrille* immediately joined the fray, sending two Ca.114 biplanes on an escort mission for the *13 Escadrille* completing a reconnaissance mission over Machala and Santa Rosa.

Meanwhile, in Quito and in the face of the overwhelming quantitative and qualitative superiority of Peruvian aerial forces, the Ecuadorean Army Aviation command decided to withdraw its available aircraft to bases in the interior.

72 EIT – After a short stay at Talara the unit landed in Tumbes, where its commander reported under the command of TON HQ and awaited further orders.

105 ET. – Transported personnel and supplies between Tumbes and Talara in support of the *41* and *42 Escadrilles*.

11 July

XI EB – The *12 Escadrille* left Talara bound for Chiclayo, where it awaited maintenance crews to complete work on the remaining aircraft on strength.

Other units registered no activity.

12 & 13 July

No aerial activity registered.

Douglas 8A-3P belonging to the *92 Escadrille, XXXI Escuadrón de Información y Ataque*, seen during its transfer flight from Lima to the operations theatre. (Sergio de la Puente Collection)

Aerial view of the town of Machala in late July 1941. (Humberto Currarino Collection)

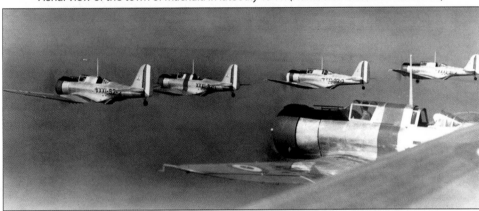

Aircraft of the XXXI EIA during their deployment from Lima to the northern border. (IEHAP)

A Douglas 8A-3P underway very low over the typical desert landscape along the Peruvian coast, on its way to the TON. (Amaru Tincopa Gallegos Collection)

A view of Santa Rosa railway station taken during one of the reconnaissance sorties by the 72 EIT. (Humberto Currarino Collection)

From right to left, 2nd Lieutenant Wensjoe, Captain Maguiña and a civilian identified as Mr Ruiz in front of a
Ca.114 fighter from *42 Escadrille*, XXI EC, in Tumbes in late July 1941. (Humberto Currarino Collection)

A line of Ca.114 fighters from *42 Escadrille*, XXI EC, at Tumbes in late July 1941. A pair of NA-50
monoplane fighters from *41 Escadrille* can be seen in the foreground. (IEHAP)

14 July

XI EB – During the early hours, the *12 Escadrille* scrambled from Chiclayo and headed north to carry out a familiarisation flight over the border. After flying along the Zarumilla and Macara sectors, the unit landed in Talara at 1130 hours. The squadron registered no further aerial activity that day.

15 July

XI EB – *12 Escadrille* continued to carry out its terrain familiarisation programme over the border. After navigating over the border, the unit landed at Tumbes airfield, where it spent the night. No additional activity was registered.

16 July

XI EB – *12 Escadrille* completed its operational training cruise, navigating between the Boca de Capones (at the mouth of the Zarumilla River) and Matapalo areas, then returning to its home base in Chiclayo. The objective of this operation was to familiarise the crews with the operational area as a preparatory step to further operations.

17 & 18 July

No aerial activity registered.

19 July

XI EB - The *11 Escadrille* left Chiclayo at 0815 hours, arriving at Talara at 0900 hours. The unit registered no additional aerial activity.

20 July

XI EB – The *11 Escadrille* flew from Talara to Tumbes forward airfield, where its commanding officer placed his unit under the command of 1 GA. No other aerial activity registered.

21 July

The 1 GA issued a number of operations orders, under the code name General Operations Order No.1, which were to be executed by all units during the early hours of 22 July.

Combat aviation was to start operations from H-hour, in cooperation with the *Primera Division Ligera* (1DL, 1st Light Division), and neutralise enemy strongpoints located at Chacras, Quebrada Seca, Rancho Chico and Huaquillas. Additionally, the aviation was to search for and neutralise any enemy troop, artillery and supply unit movement across these areas, with the secondary assignment of providing aerial coverage over the villages of Tumbes, Zarumilla, Zorritos and Talara.

On the same day, the 1 GA HQ also issued General Order of Operations No.3 containing a number of orders to be carried out by the following units:

XI EB – *12 Escadrille* was to carry out an attack on Ecuadorean Army headquarters, control posts and troop concentrations at Chacras and Huaquillas, as well as other similar objectives in Huatalco and Payana.

– *11 Escadrille* was on alert at Tumbes airfield.

XXI EC – *41 Escadrille* was to attack Ecuadorean positions near Quebrada Seca and Chacras as their primary and secondary targets, with attacks on any opportunity targets found along the road between these towns as alternative objectives.

– *42 Escadrille* was to provide air cover for the TON HQ and the neighbouring city of Tumbes, as well as provide escort to the 72 EIT units.

– *43 Escadrille* was on alert at Talara.

22 July

Due to adverse weather conditions over the operations area, the 1 GA command postponed H-hour until 0800 hours on 23 July.

23 July

XI EB (Bombardment Squadron) – A trio of *Libeccio* bombers from *12 Escadrille*, serials XI-12-1, XI-12-3 and XIV-22-3, took off from Tumbes at 0810 hours bound for Chacras to attack Ecuadorean Army ammunition depots and barracks. The aircraft carried out three bombing runs, dropping 405kg of bombs. The *11 Escadrille* also took part in the day's operations, and at 1000 hours dispatched Ca.310, serial XI-11-1, on an attack sortie against Ecuadorean positions in

The effects of an aerial attack on Ecuadorean positions near a bridge in the Matapalo region on 23 July 1941. (Amaru Tincopa Gallegos Collection)

Huaquillas. Additionally, a pair of bombers left Tumbes at 1245 hours to attack a fuel depot in Chacras, dropping 300kg of bombs and destroyinging the target.

That afternoon, the head of XI EB, Commander Humberto Gal'Lino Domenak, received orders from 1 GA command to report on the effects of the attacks performed by his unit that day. Consequently, Commander Gal'Lino took off at 1645 hours aboard Ca.310, serial XI-12-1, and carried out a photo-reconnaissance over the objectives of the day, reporting the results of the attack to HQ after landing. A pair of Ca.114 fighters from *42 Escadrille* provided escort to the single *Libeccio* for the duration of the mission.

XXI EC – While the bombers from XI EB managed to accomplish their missions without incident, the XXI EC was not so lucky, recording another loss, this time caused by direct enemy action. At 0730 hours, four NA-50 fighter-bombers from the *41 Escadrille*, each armed with two 50kg and six 15kg bombs, took off from Tumbes and headed east to attack Ecuadorean Army heavy machine-gun positions in the surrounding Quebrada Seca which were holding up the advance of Peruvian ground forces. Since the primary objectives were located in mountainous terrain, the attacking crews had to perform a shallow dive starting from their approaching height of 6,000ft in order to release their bombs. As the aircraft started their attack, the Ecuadorean positions responded with fire from heavy machine guns and small calibre weapons, hitting the NA-50 serial XXI-41-3 flown by Lieutenant José Abelardo Quiñones Gonzáles, leader of the second section, causing its fuel tank to burst into flames and the aircraft to crash, with the loss of its pilot.[4] After completing their bomb run, the remaining aircraft returned to Tumbes, where they landed at 0845 hours. On a second sortie, NA-50 XXI-41-1 and XXI-41-4, flown by Lieutenant Fernando Paraud and Commander Antonio Alberti, took off at 1100 hours bound for Chacras and Huaquillas, where

they attacked troops and vehicles on the road, returning to their base without incident.

72 EIT – In order to determine the effects of the attacks carried out by the XI EB and XXI EC during the early hours around Huaquillas, Chacras and Quebrada Seca, a reconnaissance sortie was launched by this unit at 1030 hours, with a Fairey Fox serial 72-3 under escort from a pair of Caproni Ca.114s from the *42 Escadrille*. Two hours later, another sortie was launched with the departure from Tumbes of the Fairey serial 72-2 which headed to Chacras and Arenillas. A third mission was launched at 1430 hours when the Fox serial 72-3 reconnoitred over the Ecuadorean border post at La Bomba. The unit's last mission of the day involved the crew of Fairey serial 72-1, which departed from Tumbes to perform a reconnaissance over Huaquillas and La Bomba at 1600 hours.

The loss of Lieutenant Quiñones evidenced a failure in tactics and an erroneous employment of some of the aerial units available by part of the TON command, prompting the launch of corrective actions. Consequently, 1 AG (1st Air Group) order commander-in-chief Colonel Miguel Angel Llona issued the Particular Instructive No.1 on 24 July, which transformed the 1 AG into the 1st Northern Air Group (1 NAG) by incorporating a couple of additional aerial units into its structure: the *XXXI Escuadrón de Información Estrategica y Ataque* (XXXI EIEA, XXXI Strategic Reconnaissance and Attack Squadron) and XXXII *Escuadrón de Información Maritima* (XXXII EIM, XXXII Reconnaissance Squadron of Naval Aviation).

24 July

XI EB – *12 Escadrille* launched a single patrol over Santa Rosa and Puerto Bolívar at 1015 hours. The two-aircraft formation was composed of Ca.310 XIV-23-3 and XI-12-2, which were escorted to their targets by a pair of NA-50 fighters from XXI EC.[5]

The 8A-3P had less than two years in service with the CAP when the conflict with Ecuador broke out. Equipped with dive brakes and having good performance overall, these aircraft were ideal to provide tactical support to EP troops. Incomprehensibly, the operating unit remained in Lima until 24 July, when, after the loss of a pair of NA-50 fighter bombers, the TON command finally requested its involvement in the northern theatre. (IEHAP)

The Talara Liaison Base was used as a rear maintenance centre. This photograph shows several CAP aircraft parked in front of a hangar. (Humberto Currarino Collection)

Flying the Caproni bombers were:

XIV-23-3: Lieutenant Commander Humberto Gal'Lino Domenack, pilot; 2nd Lieutenant Eduardo Montero Rojas, bomber; and Sub Officer Gonzalo Pizarro, machine gunner/radio operator.

XI-12-2: Lieutenant Commander Manuel Burgos, pilot; 2nd Lieutenant Julio Suárez Cornejo, bomber; and Sub Officer Gustavo Guerra, machine gunner.

This formation, flying at a height of 400m, reached Santa Rosa after about a 20-minute flight. Finding low clouds and strong rain over their objective, the patrol descended to 250m in order to perform a more accurate bombing run. Arenillas, their secondary target, was also covered by clouds. Consequently, the formation headed to the swamps surrounding the mouth of the Capones River in search of opportunity targets, finding some small boats, which were attacked with 15kg bombs and machine-gun fire. Upon returning to base, the crews reported a number of small boats as sunk and/or damaged.

Eight Douglas 8A-3Ps parked at Talara on 24 July 1941. (Amaru Tincopa Gallegos Collection)

CAP officers relaxing between missions. Lieutenants Rafael León de la Puente and César Lynch Cordero are holding Italian-made 15kg anti-personnel bombs, accompanied by Lieutenant Escribens (left) and 2nd Lieutenant Maurua (right). (Humberto Currarino Collection)

Another shot of the same group in Tumbes in late July 1941, this time in front of one of the two Caproni Ca.111 transports fitted as flying ambulances by Caproni Peruana personnel. (IHEAP)

Later that day, a flight comprising Ca.310 serials XI-12-1 and XI-12-2 left Tumbes at 1310 hours to attack Ecuadorean troop concentrations sighted around Chacras and Huaquillas. The aircraft, flown by Captain Pedro Aguilar (XI-12-1) and Lieutenant Otto Gastelumendi (XI-12-2), reached their target and dropped over the surprised troops a rain of 2kg anti-personnel grenades or *espezones*, reporting causing many casualties among them.[6] During the attack on their secondary objectives – government buildings in Chacras and Huaquillas landing field – a 50kg bomb became jammed in the bomb support of Ca.310 XI-12-2, and Lieutenant Gastelumendi tried several manoeuvres to set it free, without success. With no other option,

Gastelumendi brought the aircraft back to base with the bomb still in place, executing a perfectly smooth landing, after which the ground personnel carefully disarmed the device.

XXI EC – Two NA.50 from *41 Escadrille* took off from Tumbes at 1025 hours in an escort mission for XI EB units. Lieutenant Fernando Paraud, aboard NA-50 XXI-41-1, and 2nd Lieutenant Manuel Rivera López-Aliaga (XXI-41-4) provided protection for the bombers. After having completed their main assignment, during a patrol near Santa Rosa, Lieutenant Paraud discovered an Ecuadorean aircraft – probably one of the Ecuadorean Army Aviation's CW-19R – poorly camouflaged on the airfield and proceeded to attack it with machine-gun fire, setting it ablaze. Meanwhile, 2nd Lieutenant Rivera was also busy, attacking an Ecuadorean column on the Chacras-Arenillas road.

42 Escadrille also took part in an action, deploying three machines which took off from Tumbes at 1045 hours to escort Fairey serial 72-3 on an armed reconnaissance sortie over Machala, Santa Rosa, Arenilla and Chacras. After completing their assignment and while on the return trip, the fighters attacked Ecuadorean Navy (hereinafter BAE) ship *Atahualpa*, which was navigating northbound near Puerto Bolívar estuary. In the unusual encounter that followed, no victors emerged and the Peruvian pilots returned to base reporting having caused minor damage to the ship's structure. *Atahualpa's* crew, however, reported a grossly magnified outcome, and the media in Quito and Guayaquil asserted that the ship's crew had shot down at least one Peruvian aircraft.[7]

The *escadrille* launched another sortie shortly after, consisting of a single-aircraft patrol for the Fairey 72-2 reporting automotive traffic along the Chacras-Arenillas road. This mission began at 1230 hours, led by Captain David Roca aboard Ca.114 XXI-42-1. After completing his primary mission and while looking for opportunity targets in the Chacras area, Captain Roca discovered a truck loaded with Ecuadorean troops, strafing it before returning to Tumbes at 1315 hours. At 1430 hours, a two-airplane patrol composed of Capronis XXI-42-1 and XXI-42-3 took off to protect the Fairey serial 72-3 during a reconnaissance mission over the Ecuadorean vigilance post at La Bomba. After completing their duties, both fighters returned to Tumbes at 1510 hours. Twenty minutes later, 2nd Lieutenant CAP José Winder took off aboard XXI-42-2 on a mission to escort two Ca.310 bombers from *12 Escadrille* attacking an Ecuadorean Army post at Huaquillas. Flying at an average height of 1,600m, Winder noted the absence of the Ecuadorean aviation and returned to Tumbes after an 80-minute flight. At 1600 hours, the Caproni XXI-42-3 took off on an escort mission for Fairey 72-1, which was heading to the area between Huaquillas and La Bomba to report Ecuadorean army movements in the area. The squadron's last mission of the day was launched at 1645 hours, consisting of a two-aircraft formation escorting a Ca.310 bomber heading to Puerto Bolívar to attack Ecuadorean shipping reported in the area. The formation returned to base an hour later.

XXXI EIA – After a short stay in Talara, the unit arrived at Tumbes forward airfield at 1230 hours and started operations immediately, deploying all its *escadrilles* on a familiarisation flight over the operational area, following the Tumbes-Cuenca and Tumbes-Loja axis. For this purpose, they were supported by a Ca.310 from XI EB which served as formation guide.

At 1430 hours, the *91 Escadrille* departed from Tumbes bound for Piura, carrying the TON and 1st Air Group commanders. The unit and passengers spent the night at Piura.

72 EIT – Fox 72-3, piloted by Lieutenant Carlos Márquez and Lieutenant Alférez Francisco Cavero, performed a reconnaissance mission over the road between Chacras and Arenillas, reporting that it was unusable due to heavy shelling and bombardment.

A nice in-flight study of Vought V-80P Corsair serial XXXII-83-2 flown by Lieutenant Heighnes Perez Albela during the transfer of elements from XXXII EIM from their base in Ancón to the operations theatre. (Humberto Currarino Collection)

Chimbote Bay, 27 July 1941. Rough water upon landing caused damage to the floats of Curtiss Cyclone Falcon XXXII-82-2, which soon began to take on water and became semi-submerged. BAP *Urubamba* arrived on the scene in order to retrieve the aircraft, which was later taken back to Ancon where it was repaired. Meanwhile, Falcon 82-1, whose tail plane was also damaged, arrived ashore by its own means and ground crews proceeded immediately to perform the necessary repairs. (Humberto Currarino Collection)

At 1450 hours on 27 July, the Curtiss Falcon 82-3 joined the *escadrille* at Chimbote, being refuelled and stationed at the beach while its crew awaited the repairs on XXXII-82-1 to be completed. (Humberto Currarino Collection)

A curious crowd gathering around the Falcon XXXII-82-1 after its arrival in Chimbote. (Amaru Tincopa Gallegos Collection).

25 July

XI EB – A patrol of two *Libeccios*, composed of Ca.310 serial XI-12-1 flown by Captain Pedro Aguilar, 2nd Lieutenant Teobaldo Gonzalez and 2nd Sub Officer Juan Oyola, and XI-12-3 flown by Lieutenant Teodomiro Gabilondo, 2nd Lieutenant Jorge Calmell del Solar and 1st Sub Officer German Vergara, took off from Tumbes at 1240 hours to attack Ecuadorean military targets discovered near Puerto Bolivar and Arenillas. Arriving over Puerto Bolívar at a height of 1,600m, the formation discovered the target covered by low clouds so decided to decrease their altitude, carrying out a bombing run at 500m and without the aids of the Jozza U-3 type bombsight. The weather was even worse over Arenillas, meaning objectives in that area could not be attacked.

XXI EC – This formation received orders to displace its units on a patrol mission over the Puerto Bolívar and Jambeli channel area, looking to attract AE units into combat. A secondary mission included searching for the "Ecuadorean fleet", supposedly positioned outside Puerto Bolívar.

Complying with the directives issued by the command, *41 Escadrille* launched a patrol comprising North American XXI-41-1, XXI-41-4 and XXI-41-5 flown by Lieutenant Fernando Paraud,

Commander Lieutenant Antonio Alberti and 2nd Lieutenant Manuel Rivera, respectively. This formation departed from Tumbes at 1245 hours and headed north towards Santa Rosa and Guayaquil, and arriving over their objectives at a height of 3,000m reported a total absence of Ecuadorean aircraft.

Meanwhile, the *42 Escadrille* also launched several sorties. The first was a reconnaissance mission between Chacras and Arenillas flown by 2nd Lieutenant Jose Winder aboard Ca.114 XXI-42-2, who reported no Ecuadorean Army movement in the area. The second sortie took place at 1350 hours and was performed by 2nd Lieutenant Cesar Garces flying Caproni XXI-42-3 escorting a Fairey Fox from 72 EIT tasked to bomb Ecuadorean positions around Huatalco. A third sortie for the day was performed by Captain David Roca and 2nd Lieutenant Cesar Garces aboard Ca.114s serials XXI-42-1 and XXI-42-3, respectively, who patrolled the air space over Tumbes. The fourth sortie was an escort mission on behalf of 72 EIT aircraft bound for Chacras and Santa Rosa, and was flown by 2nd Lieutenant Cesar Garces aboard Caproni 42-2. The day's last sortie was performed by Captain David Roca and 2nd Lieutenant Cesar Garces, who took off at 1635 hours on a reconnaissance mission over the Jambeli channel aboard Capronis XXI-42-1 and XXI-42-3.

Four 8A-3Ps during a reconnaissance flight over the Ecuadorian lines at the end of July 1941. (Amaru Tincopa Gallegos Collection)

XXXI EIA – *91 Escadrille* mobilised from Piura to Tumbes forward airfield.

72 EIT – Fox IV serial 72-1 took off from Tumbes at 1025 hours under the command of Lieutenant Francisco García Romero, tasked to perform a reconnaissance over the Huaquillas-Huatalco road, with the secondary objective to attack opportunity targets discovered in the area. During their return flight, 2nd Lieutenant Raul Pinillos, his gunner-observer, saw EP cavalry troops on the Zarumilla-Aguas Verdes road. On the second mission of the day, Lieutenant Carlos Marquez flew Fairey 72-3 with 2nd Lieutenant Dante Monge as observer, overflying the Chacras-Arenillas road and Arenilla-Santa Rosa railroad, attacking opportunity targets around Arenillas as well as reporting anti-aircraft artillery activity near Santa Rosa. At the latter location their aircraft was shaken by the impact of a 20mm shell that exploded near the starboard wing and ripped some of the lower wing fabric. Finally, during the third sortie of the day, Lieutenant Francisco García Romero and his observer, 2nd Lieutenant Raúl Pinillos, performed an armed reconnaissance over Huatalco, Arenillas and Santa Rosa aboard Fairey Fox serial 72-1, obtaining valuable photographic images as well as attacking machine-gun nests discovered near Huatalco.

26 July

XI EB – No air activity registered.

XXI EC – A patrol composed of North American NA-50 serials XXI-41-1 and XXI-41-4, flown by Lieutenant Commander Antonio Alberti and Lieutenant Fernando Paraud, respectively, took off from Tumbes at 0730 hours, heading north to Santa Rosa to intercept an unidentified aircraft spotted by Peruvian troops over that area. The formation arrived only to find that the aircraft had abandoned the

area, and returned to Tumbes after 45 minutes in the air. Meanwhile, the *42 Escadrille* made two escort sorties on benefit of 72 EIT. The first sortie began at 1130 hours, when Ca.114 serials XXI-42-2 and XXI-42-3 took off from Tumbes to escort a Fairey biplane from 72 EIT on a reconnaissance mission over Ecuadorean territory. During the return, both fighters attacked opportunity targets near Arenillas and Santa Rosa. A second sortie took a pair of Ca.114s on a patrol between Tumbes and Boca Capones, escorting a Fox IV from 72 EIT.

XXXI EIA – The *92* and *93 Escadrilles* flew from Chiclayo to Talara during the early morning. At Talara, the *92 Escadrille* commander received orders from 1st Light Division's commander to perform an armed reconnaissance over La Tina-Macará-Carlamanga-Gozanaba-Alamor-Zapotillo-Célica-Huancha, departing at 1145 hours and returning an hour-and-a-half later. During the debriefing, the *escadrille* leader, Captain Enrique Bernales, reported Ecuadorean forces were completely absent in these areas.

XXXII EIM – The unit began its deployment to the operations area at dawn, with its ground echelon departing from Ancon base.[8] This group arrived at Chimbote the same day and stationed waiting for the arrival of the flying echelon.[9]

72 EIT – The increased activity shown by Ecuadorean forces in different sectors of the frontier give the TON command hints of an impending counter-attack. Therefore, and in order to gather better intelligence about the composition and magnitude of Ecuadorean units facing the Peruvian Army's advance, an armed reconnaissance mission was launched to discover any signs of Ecuadorean troops and vehicles between Chacras-Arenillas-Sauce villages, Arenillas-Santa Rosa, Arenillas-Pitahaya, as well as on the road from Pitahaya to Cayanca and Huaquillas. This mission was carried out by Lieutenant Marquez and 2nd Lieutenant Muñiz, who took off from Tumbes

An unidentified airman from the XI EB next to a line of Ca.310 bombers from the *11 Escadrille* at Talara in late July 1941. (Amaru Tincopa Gallegos Collection)

Personnel from the ground echelon of XXXII EIM next to the Curtiss serial XXXII-82-1, which was undergoing routine maintenance at Puerto Pizarro forward base, Tumbes, in late July 1941. (Amaru Tincopa Gallegos Collection)

aboard the Fairey 72-2 at 1130 hours, returning two hours later without incident after obtaining valuable images of the Quebrada de Salinas, Bejucal, Arenillas and Cayanca areas.

On a second mission, Lieutenant García Romero took off from Tumbes aboard 72-1 carrying EP Commander Cesar Eguisquiza as observer. The aircraft overflew the Tumbes-Zarumilla-Chacras-Carcabón-Arenillas-Santa Rosa-Machala-Pasaje-Puerto Bolívar-Boca Capones-Puerto Pizarro areas, escorted by two Ca.114s from *42 Escadrille*.

Peruvian troops near Santa Rosa reported a large Ecuadorean aircraft landing at the airfield located in the city's outskirts on 26 July. This aircraft was almost certainly Ju-52 *Azuay*, which flew there from Guayaquil carrying officers, equipment and documents. The cautious crew of *Azuay*, afraid of being discovered by the almost omnipresent CAP aircraft, took off immediately after unloading their cargo.

Crews of the *11 Escadrille* formed in front of their aircraft during a review prior to the start of a new day of operations. (Amaru Tincopa Gallegos Collection)

27 July

XI EB – No aerial activity was registered.

XXI EC – No activity registered.

XXXI EIA – A pair of Douglas 8A-3Ps took off from Tumbes to carry out an armed reconnaissance

Ground crews from XI EB while rearming their Ca.310 bombers in Talara in late July 1941. (Amaru Tincopa Gallegos Collection)

mission over Puerto Bolívar, Machala, Pasaje, San Sebastián, Santa Isabel, Asunción, Girón and Tarqui. For its secondary objective, the formation flew to Uzcurrumi village to determine the nature and composition of the bridge that crossed the Jubones River in order to gather information for a future attack. The mission was flown by Captain Enrique Ciriani and Sub Officer Juan Hernández aboard 8A-3P serial XXXI-91-1and Lieutenant Jesús Melgar and 2nd Lieutenant Enrique Debernardi aboard XXXI-92-2.

XXXII EIM – The flying echelon of the *82 Escadrille*, comprising a trio of Curtiss model 37F Cyclone Falcons, took off from Ancon at 0910 hours. Aboard the aircraft were Captain Augusto Duarte as pilot and Sub Officer Anastacio Velázquez as machine gunner/observer aboard XXXII-82-1; 2nd Lieutenant Alberto López C. as pilot and Sub Officer Manuel Eyzaguirre as machine gunner/mechanic on XXXII-82-2; and pilot 2nd Lieutenant Ernesto Fernandez accompanied by SubOfficer master mechanic Julio Flores flying XXXII-82-3. The start of the operation, as part of TON, was not favourable for this unit: just 15 minutes after take-off, XXXII-82-3 was forced to make an emergency landing on water near Huarmey harbour due to a problem with the engine fuel feeding system. While the mechanic on board fixed the problem, the two remaining machines continued their journey north, arriving at Chimbote at 1205 hours after brief stops in Supe, Huarmey

and Casma. The ground echelon of this unit, which had departed Ancón the previous evening, was already in position and awaiting the arrival of the aircraft at Chimbote, having placed buoys and boats on the bay in order to refuel the aircraft. Both Falcons, however, became damaged upon landing due to the rough sea conditions, with XXXII-82-1 sustaining damage to its tail plane while XXXII-82-2 suffered holes in its floats and ended semi-submerged soon after. The latter was rescued by the crew of BAP *Urubamba*, which used a crane to recover the aircraft and transport it back to Ancón for repairs. In the meantime, Cyclone Falcon XXXII-82-1 had arrived ashore by its own means, and ground crews proceeded immediately to perform the necessary repairs to its structure. A couple of hours later, after completing the required fix and repairs, Curtiss Cyclone Falcon serial XXXII-82-3 joined the *escadrille* at Chimbote at 1450 hours. It was immediately refuelled and stationed on the beach, where it waited for the ground crews to complete the repairs on XXXII-82-1.

72 EIT – No air activity registered.

28 July

At Tumbes and other air fields, personnel from all units held ceremonies celebrating the anniversary of Peruvian independence.

XI EB – A two-aircraft patrol from *12 Escadrille* – Ca.310 XIV-

A Grumman G-21 Goose from the *101 Escuadrilla*, 51 EA, moored at Cabo Pantoja in the western Amazon. This unit provided transport and liaison services between Lima and dozens of garrisons scattered across the vast Amazon Basin. (Amaru Tincopa Gallegos Collection)

23-3 flown by Commander Lieutenant Humberto Gal'Lino, and XI-12-2 by Lieutenant Marcial Burgos – took off from Tumbes at 1130 hours and headed for Puerto Bolívar, reaching the target 20 minutes later at a height of 2,000m. However, due to adverse meteorological conditions in the area, the bombers were only able to perform a single bomb run, diverting to Machala in order to attack opportunity targets. A second sortie from *12 Escadrille* was launched against Santa Rosa, with alternative targets in Machala. The patrol was composed of *Libeccios* XI-12-1, flown by Captain Pedro Aguilar, and XI-12-3, commanded by Lieutenant Teodomiro Gabilondo. Both bombers, however, were unable to attack their intended targets due to the presence of heavy fog over Santa Rosa, so instead moved westwards to attack secondary objectives in Machala, Puerto Bolívar and Pasaje. A third sortie was flown by Lieutenant Rafael León de la Fuente aboard Ca.310 serial XIV-22-1, which, took off from Tumbes at 1205 hours to attack a bridge near the town of Uzcurrumi. This mission was claimed a success by Lieutenant de la Fuente, who reported that his bombs caused heavy damage to the structure, rendering it useless for traffic. The fourth sortie of the day was launched at 1435 hours, flown by Lieutenant Otto Gastelumendi aboard Ca.310 serial XI-11-2, who flew his aircraft on an attack mission against targets around Santa Rosa. A fifth sortie, flown by Lieutenant Teodomiro Gabilondo who took off at 1620 hours aboard *Libeccio* 12-3, attacked a railroad bridge located between Machala and Santa Rosa, but the objective could not be accomplished due to dense mist covering the area. Finally, Lieutenant Marcial Burgos took off at 1730 hours aboard aircraft XI-12-2 for the last mission of the day, heading to Machala to attack the train station, which was heavily damaged.

XXI EC – A three-aircraft patrol from *41 Escadrille* flew to Guayaquil, dropping propaganda leaflets from a height of 3,000m. The mission was performed at that height to avoid the dense AA fire surrounding the city.

XXXI EIA – No activity registered.

XXXII EIM – Curtiss XXXII-82-1 and XXXII-82-3 left Chimbote at 1400 hours. They arrived over Chiclayo at a height of 2,000m and continued north towards Bayovar and Talara, finally arriving at Puerto Pizarro at 1812 hours.

72 EIT – Following the guidelines of Operation Order No.20, Lieutenant García Romero took off from Tumbes at 0545 hours to perform an armed reconnaissance over Matapalo Island aboard Fairey 72-1, carrying 2nd Lieutenant Hartwig Holler as observer. During the course of this mission, several Ecuadorean Army positions were attacked with 50kg bombs and machine-gun fire before returning to base at 0715 hours. Once rearmed and refuelled, the aircraft took off again at 1015 hours – again under Lieutenant García Romero but this time carrying 2nd Lieutenant Muñiz as observer. This sortie was again directed to Matapalo Island, where the crew verified that MGP landing craft were already disembarking Peruvian Army troops. Finally, and in accordance with the contents of Supplementary Mission Order No.2, Fairey 72-1, flown by Lieutenant García Romero and EP Captain Alfredo Novoa, performed a reconnaissance over Tumbes-Zarumilla-Chacras-Carcabón-Arenillas-Santa Rosa-Machala-Pasaje-Puerto Bolívar-Boca de Capones-Puerto Pizarro, returning to Tumbes without incident.

29 July

XI EB – The *11* and *12 Escadrilles* launched several sorties directed to attack supply routes in the rear of the Ecuadorean lines, including the railroad bridge between Arenillas and Santa Rosa, the Arenillas train station, the Uzcurrumi railroad bridge and the railroad bridge between Santa Rosa and Machala.

XXI EC – Three NA-50s fighter-bombers from *41 Escadrille* performed a reconnaissance over Guayaquil, where they dropped propaganda leaflets.

XXXI EIA – *91 Escadrille* attacked the railroad bridge over the Arenillas River as well as Ecuadorean Army positions around the village of Chacras.

XXXII EIM – After arriving in Puerto Pizarro and with its ground staff, fuel and supplies in place, the *82 Escadrille* began launching operations under TON command, with the first sortie a patrol over the gulf of Guayaquil carried out by Cyclone Falcons serials XXXII-82-1 and XXXII-82-3. The aircraft, flown by Captain Duarte and 2nd

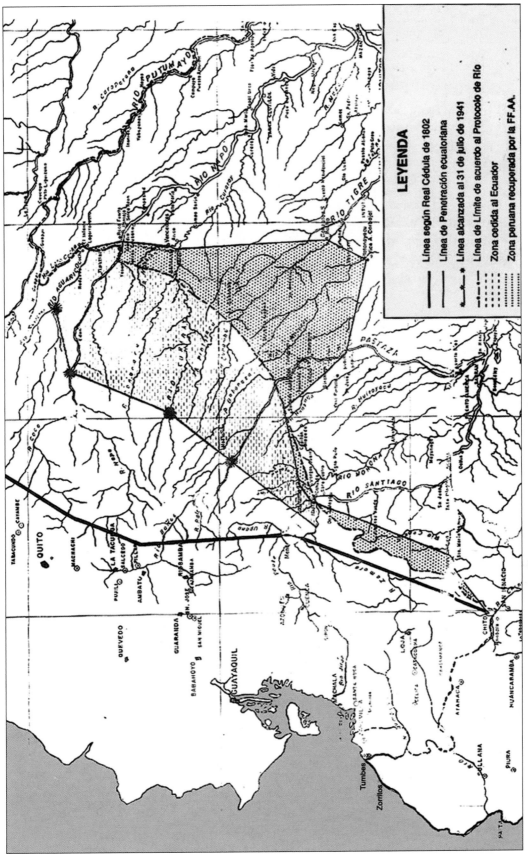

Map of the major combat zone, as seen by the Peruvians. The thick black line indicates the border between Ecuador and Peru as determined by the *Real Cédula* of 1802. The dotted area to the south-east shows the outer limits of the Ecuadorean advance in early 1941, while the line in between them indicates the final positions reached by Peruvians during their counteroffensive that ended on 31 July 1941. (IEHAP via author)

Civilian and military personnel in front of one of the 8A-3P from the XXXI EIA at Talara during a pause in operations. (Amaru Tincopa Gallegos Collection)

Aircraft from XXXI EIA prepare to depart Talara, where the unit arrived as part of the crew familiarisation flights. (IEHAP)

Lieutenant Lañas accompanied by mechanics Sub Officers Flores and Vasquez, respectively, left Puerto Pizarro and headed north, arriving over Guayaquil at a height of 2,000m, taking oblique photographs of the city's harbour and anchorage, then heading to Santa Rosa-Puerto Bolívar-Puerto Pizarro, at an average height of 500m, before returning to base. After completing this sortie, the crews reported the sighting of four Ecuadorean Navy ships anchored at Guayaquil and attacks on two large barges carrying troops sailing north outside Punta Mondragón. The patrol also reported the presence of Peruvian fighters patrolling Guayaquil at a height of 3,000m.

72 EIT – Fairey 72-1, commanded by Lieutenant García Romero accompanied by 2nd Lieutenant Raúl Pinillos as observer, took off at 1015 hours bound for Santa Rosa to take photos of the village of

Cayanca, the Pitahaya army post and the road leading from there to Santa Rosa. During the flight, the aviators observed that the Ecuadorean post at Pitahaya was already under the control of Peruvian forces. Later, at 1130 hours, Lieutenant Carlos Marquez and 2nd Lieutenant Francisco Cavero took off aboard Fairey 72-3 to perform a photographic reconnaissance over Chacras, Arenillas, Pitahaya and Dos Bocas villages. Finally, at 1240 hours, Fairey 72-3 took to the skies for a new sortie – again piloted by Lieutenant Marquez but this time carrying 2nd Lieutenant Dante Monge as observer. Upon returning, they reported the presence of EP army tents near Arenillas as well as the effects of the attack performed by XI EB on Puerto Bolívar.

Aircraft and crews from 72 EIT during operations from Tumbes forward airfield. (Amaru Tincopa Gallegos Collection)

30 July

XI EB – The *11 Escadrille*, stationed at Talara, replaced *12 Escadrille* in Tumbes. After completing its transfer, the unit began operations at 1630 hours with a sortie flown by Lieutenant Cayo Murillo, carrying Captain Ravines, 2nd Lieutenant Kisic and Sub Officer Granadino as crew, aboard *Libeccio* serial XI-11-3. Murillo and his crew attacked the hills around Arenillas, where the 72 EIT reported the presence of machine-gun nests hindering the advance of Peruvian ground forces. After dropping four 50kg bombs over several targets, Lieutenant Cayo directed his aircraft over Chacras, reporting vehicles abandoned along the route leading from Chacras to Arenillas. The unit's second sortie was flown by Captain Humberto Buenaño and a crew composed of Lieutenant Bernardino Valencia (bomber), Lieutenant Teobaldo Gonzalez (observer) and 2nd Sub Officer Federico Bustamante (artillery officer) aboard *Libeccio* XI-11-1. They took off at 1730 hours to attack targets around Santa Rosa. After landing, Captain Buenaño

reported some bullet impacts on his aircraft caused by heavy small-calibre anti-aircraft fire near Santa Rosa.

XXI EC – The *42 Escadrille* was replaced by *43 Escadrille*, which was stationed at Talara forward airfield on alert.

XXXI EIA – The *92 Escadrille* deployed a pair of 8A-3Ps on a reconnaissance sortie inside Ecuadorean territory. The Douglas serials XXXI-92-1 and XXXI-92-3 flew over the Pasaje-Quebrada-Río Jubones-Girón-Tarqui-Cuenca axis looking for signs of Ecuadorean forces. This mission was successfully completed, both machines strafing trucks carrying Ecuadorean troops travelling from Giron to Tarqui.

XXXII EIM – Captain Duarte departed from Puerto Pizarro at 0830 hours accompanied by 2nd Lieutenant Fernandez Lañas aboard Falcon XXXII-82-1, performing a reconnaissance over the Puerto Pizarro-Guayaquil coastline, returning to base at 1150 hours. During debriefing, the officers reported that Puerto Bolívar and Machala

Another view of the men assigned to XI EB in a more relaxed portrait with one of the units' aircraft at Tumbes in late 1941. (Amaru Tincopa Gallegos Collection)

A nice view of XXXII EIM aircraft moored at the Puerto Pizarro estuary, a forward operative base located near Tumbes and the operations zone. (Amaru Tincopa Gallegos Collection)

seemed abandoned and that a transport ship bearing a Chilean flag had entered Guayaquil bay. A similar mission was performed that afternoon by 2nd Lieutenant Fernandez and Sub Officer Flores.

72 EIT – Lieutenant Garcia Romero and 2nd Lieutenant Hernan Muñiz departed aboard Fairey 72-1 at 0915 hours in a reconnaissance sortie to take photographs of Puerto Bolívar and its surroundings, confirming the absence of Ecuadorean troops in the area. During the return trip, the crew discovered two Ecuadorean Army vehicles at Huaquillas and attacked them. A second sortie was flown by Lieutenant Marquez and 2nd Lieutenant Monge aboard Fairey 72-2 at 1145 hours. After returning, both reported that no Ecuadorean forces could be located in Arenillas or Santa Rosa. Finally, Fairey 72-2 departed again, this time commanded by Lieutenant Marquez who, together with 2nd Lieutenant Pinillos, reported to the TON command the advance of Peruvian vehicles on the road to Arenillas.

July 31

XI EB – Caproni serial XIV-23-3, flown by Commander Humberto Gal'Lino, took off from Tumbes at 1110 hours to carry out a reconnaissance cruise over Santa Rosa, Machala and Puerto Bolívar in order to verify the effects of CAP attacks on these cities.

XXI EC – The *41 Escadrille* sent NA-50 serials XXI-41-1 and XXI-41-4 on three sorties directed against Ecuadorean positions near Machala and Santa Rosa. In the meantime, the *43 Escadrille* launched

three sorties: an armed reconnaissance over Santa Rosa performed by Ca.114 XXI-43-1 and 43-3; an escort flight for a Ca.111 from 105 ET by Ca.114 serial XXI-43-2; and an escort mission for another Ca.111 from 105 ET by three Ca.114s.

XXXI EIA – After an urgent request from the TON commander, *93 Escadrille* flew to Piura and from there performed several close-support sorties against Ecuadorean troop strongpoints in Macará, Loja, Célica and Huachamana. The missions were successful, but the Ecuadorean troops near Loja offered fierce resistance and Douglas XXXI-93-3 was struck by several bullets. Meanwhile, the *92 Escadrille* performed an armed reconnaissance sortie over Puerto Bolívar, where a pair of barges carrying Ecuadorean equipment and troops were discovered and attacked. Likewise, a number of Ecuadorean effectives mobilising from Pasaje towards Giron were identified and attacked with bombs and machine-gun fire.

XXXII EIM – A pair of Curtiss Cyclone Falcons with serials XXXII-82-1 and XXXII-82-2, flown by Captain Duarte (with 2nd Frigate Lieutenant Oscar Mavila as observer) and 2nd Lieutenant Lañas (carrying 2nd Frigate Lieutenant Jorge Corpancho), respectively, took off from their forward base in Puerto Pizarro at 0745 hours, heading north to perform an armed reconnaissance over Santa Rosa, Guayaquil, Boca de Capones, Isla Payana, Jambelí, Puerto Puná, Guayas, Puerto Durand and Isla Manglarcitos before returning to Puerto Pizarro. The sortie lasted for two-and-a-half hours. Another sortie was flown at

1450 hours by Captain Duarte, accompanied by 2nd Frigate Lieutenant Corpancho, aboard Cyclone Falcon XXXII-82-1. They reported the absence of naval activity in the seas near Guayaquil, but the presence of metal-topped *"chatas"* carrying Ecuadorean troops near Balao and Truquel.[10]

72 EIT – The Fairey Fox serial 72-3, flown by Lieutenant Marquez and 2nd Lieutenant Cavero, took off from Tumbes at 0830 hours, heading to Chacras and Arenilla to observe the advance of Peruvian troops on the highway connecting these villages. A second sortie over Santa Rosa was ordered and launched at 0940 hours when Fairey 72-1 took off from Tumbes, flown by Lieutenant Garcia Romero and 2nd Lieutenant Hartwig Holler. On this mission, a number of oblique photographs of the train station were taken. Finally, at 1430 hours, a two-aircraft patrol composed of the Fairey Fox 72-1, flown by Lieutenant Garcia Romero and 2nd Sub Officer Boero, as well as 72-2, flown by Lieutenant Marquez and Sub Officer Hipolito Paredes, flew to Santa Rosa, landing at this city's landing strip, which had just been occupied by Peruvian forces.

105 ET – This unit flew several supply sorties between Tumbes and objectives in Ecuadorean territory for EP ground troops, parachutists and army staff in a series of operations.

The main square of Santa Rosa after the town was secured by Peruvian forces on 31 July. (Amaru Tincopa Gallegos Collection)

Tragically, Peruvian air strikes with incendiaries and the lack of fire-fighters caused a massive conflagration that gutted most of Santa Rosa, where the majority of buildings were made of wood. (Amaru Tincopa Gallegos Collection)

The airborne "assault" and the capture of Puerto Bolívar

Poorly equipped and organised, Ecuadorean forces – despite some valiant attempts at counter-attack between 26 and 29 July – eventually crumbled under the combined weight of the Peruvian offensive and, by the evening of 30 July, began a disorganised withdrawal, chased closely by EP forces.

In the diplomatic field, the Ecuadorean government agreed to take part in peace talks sponsored by neighbouring countries, and accepted a ceasefire which was scheduled to come into effect at 1800 hours on 31 July.[11] Aware of this situation, TON command ordered the planning and execution of a series of operations to capture the cities of Machala, Santa Rosa and Puerto Bolívar, which – although

unprotected – were still in no man's land. Accordingly, the command considered the use of transport aircraft to ferry small groups of troops quickly to these targets to capture them before the ceasefire began. They also considered the limited use of paratroopers in the case of Puerto Bolívar, which did not have an airfield.

After rapid but careful planning, the operation began at 1030 hours as Lieutenant Commander Antonio Rojas Cadillo, commander of the 105 ET, issued a request to the 1 GA command for the provision of aerial escorts and close support from the XI, XXI, XXXI and XXXII Squadrons.

With authorisation to begin the operation, at 1145 hours the Caproni Ca.111, serial 105-2, flown by Lieutenant Teodomiro Gabilondo and 2nd Lieutenant Luis Benavides Milera, took off from

Another view of the centre of Santa Rosa after its destruction by fire. (Amaru Tincopa Gallegos Collection)

Lieutenant León de La Fuente poses in front of his aircraft. Note the improvised wheel covers, used to prevent tyre damage from hot oil dripping from the engine. (Humberto Currarino Collection)

Aerial view of the pier at Puerto Bolívar after the town was secured by Peruvian troops. This photograph was taken by the crew of a Cyclone Falcon from the XXXII EIM. (Amaru Tincopa Gallegos Collection)

A close-up from the same photograph, showing the Peruvian Navy's *P-101* and *P-102* patrol boats and an unidentified steamer already moored within the small harbour of Puerto Bolívar. Note the presence of numerous ammunition boxes and weapons abandoned by the withdrawing Ecuadorean troops. (Amaru Tincopa Gallegos Collection)

Tumbes bound for Santa Rosa, carrying eight CAP ground troops armed with rifles and automatic weapons. These men, led by Captain Raúl Ravines, were to secure the small airstrip at Santa Rosa in order to allow reinforcements to fly in safely. Leading 2nd Lieutenant Benavides' aircraft was Lieutenant García Romero aboard a Fairey Fox IV, serial 72-3. Lieutenant Romero served as pathfinder to the transport pilot, who was unfamiliar with the terrain, to ensure a safe arrival of the transport at Santa Rosa.

Both aircraft arrived over the target at 1200 hours and, after landing, Captain Ravines climbed out of the port access door of the Caproni transport, shouting "Viva el Peru!", followed closely by his men. After the last soldier left the aircraft, Lieutenant Gabilondo took the big transport into the air again and headed back to Tumbes, where he picked up another group of 10 CAP ground troops, carrying them to

Santa Rosa to reinforce Captain Ravines' position. In the meantime, a pair of Faireys from the 72 EIT had landed in Santa Rosa shortly after its capture by Peruvian forces, with their crews joining the defence of the airfield.

A second mission responded to Operations Memos No.9 and 10, calling for the capture of Machala and Puerto Bolívar with airborne troops and paratroopers supported by combat aviation. To accomplish this, a Caproni Ca.111, serial 105-1, under the command of Lieutenant Commander Antonio Rojas Cadillo, with Lieutenant Jaime Cayo Murillo as co-pilot, took off from Tumbes at 1640 hours. They had a cargo of 10 CAP troops composed of six CAP soldiers led by Master Sub Officer Adolfo Granadino, and three paratroopers, 1st Sub Officer Antonio Brandariz Ulloa, 2nd Sub Officer Carlos Raffo García and 3rd Sub Officer Armando Orozco Falla. While the ground

Tumbes, 31 July 1941: troops form before boarding one of the Ca.111s that would transport them to the Ecuadorean airfields of Santa Rosa and Machala. (IEHAP)

CAP airborne troops boarding transports before the start of operations to capture Santa Rocha, Machala and Puerto Bolívar. (Amaru Tincopa Gallegos Collection)

A rare aerial view of three CAP paratroopers as they descend towards Puerto Bolívar. (IEHAP)

Tumbes, 31 July 1941: Lieutenants León de la Fuente, Escribens and Lynch in front of a
line of 8A-3Ps from XXXI EIA. (Humberto Currarino Collection)

Shortly after their landing and after the harbour was secured, the paratroopers received assistance
from the crew of Cyclone Falcon XXXII-82-3. (Amaru Tincopa Gallegos Collection)

troops were tasked with the capture of the landing strip at Machala, the paratroopers' mission was to capture Puerto Bolívar, a few kilometres west of Machala, and await the arrival of Peruvian ground forces. After a 20-minute flight from Tumbes, the big transport aircraft, under the protection of elements from XXI and XXXI Squadrons, landed in a field outside Machala where it left the six troops, commanded by Sub Officer Granadino. After some last-minute checks, the transport took off again at 1745 hours, heading west and climbing in order to reach sufficient altitude to launch the paratroopers over the nearby objective. Bad weather, however, forced the pilot to make a second pass at lower height. Therefore, 15 minutes after Machala's capture, paratroopers jumped off the transport, and two of them landed without trouble, but a third was blown off-course by strong winds, fell into nearby mangroves and had to be helped out of his predicament

by local anglers. After regrouping, the men awaited the arrival of 1st Light Division forces that were advancing towards their position from Machala.

Hours later, a close inspection of the captured docks revealed a sizeable stock of military supplies and weapons abandoned by Ecuadorean forces during their withdrawal. Among these were guns, helmets, ammunition of different calibres and four 20mm Breda *Cannone-Mitragliera da 20/65 modello 35* anti-aircraft cannons.

Such a small number of paratroopers were employed during this operation because intelligence reports had confirmed the complete absence of Ecuadorean opposition in the area. The real objective of the mission was to grab and keep possession of Puerto Bolívar before the ceasefire came into effect.

5

PERUVIAN COMBAT OPERATIONS FROM AUGUST 1941 UNTIL THE END OF THE CONFLICT

While military actions by both sides officially ended at 1800 hours on 31 July, as per the ceasefire organised by Argentina, Brazil, Chile and the United States of America, operations continued, although on a reduced scale, during the following two months over the occupied territories of El Oro province in southern Ecuador when another front opened as military actions became active along the Napo River in the TONO. The following is a résumé of the main aerial operations during this period. Documentation of the Peruvian Air Force General Orders for the Year 1941 contains the following entries for August and subsequent months.

1 August

In accordance with the ceasefire agreement that entered into effect the previous day, the CAP had to restrict its activities to patrols over occupied territory. However, a number of missions over the Ecuadorean coastline and the Guayaquil gulf were made, despite the evident provocation that these flights could cause to the Ecuadoreans.

Following Mission Order No.8 and Memorandum 7-A, the missions flown at this time were as follows:

XI EB – No aerial activity was registered.

XXI EC – 41 Escadrille launched two sorties to Machala and Puerto Bolívar, one in the morning and another in the afternoon. 42 Escadrille launched two aircraft on a reconnaissance sweep over Machala and 43 Escadrille sent an aircraft to Machala landing strip, where it found the Caproni Ca.111 serial 105-1 which had crashed during take-off there.

XXXI EIA – Two aircraft from 92 Escadrille took off from Tumbes to cover troop landings in Machala and Puerto Bolívar.

XXXII EIM – This squadron launched two sorties, the first flown by Captain Duarte and 2nd Frigate Lieutenant Oscar Davila, who took off from Puerto Pizarro at 0905 hours aboard Falcon XXXII-82-1, heading north to reconnoitre over Puerto Bolívar. This mission, however, had to be aborted shortly afterwards due to poor weather conditions. The second sortie was flown under better meteorological conditions by 2nd Lieutenant Ernesto Fernández and 2nd Frigate Lieutenant Oscar Corpancho in Cyclone Falcon XXXII-82-3, who flew following the coastline all the way up to the Jambeli River mouth, returning over Motorilos island, Balaos, Tendales, Machala, Santa Rosa and Puerto Bolívar, taking oblique photographs of these two last villages in the process.

72 EIT – Two aircraft performed a number of liaison flights carrying officers

from the EP 5th Infantry Battalion between Santa Rosa and Machala on 1, 2, 3 and 4 August.

105 ET – This formation began to ferry Army troops from Santa Rosa to Machala aboard Ca.111 105-2 and 105-3.

2 August

XI EB – No air activity registered.

XXI EC – Each of its units launched two sorties over Machala and Santa Rosa, providing escorts to the transports from 105 ET.

XXXI EIA – Performed two reconnaissance sorties: the first over the Pasaje-Jirón-Portete-Tarqui axis and the second over the Piura-Quebrada Cazaderos region.

XXXII EIM – At 1105 hours and during the course of a patrol over the mangroves surrounding Puerto Bolívar, Cyclone Falcon serial XXXII-82-3, flown by 2nd Lieutenant Fernández and 2nd Frigate Lieutenant Corpancho, discovered a sailing boat that was trying to escape the Peruvian blockade, forcing its captain to return to harbour. In the meantime, Vought V-80P serial XXXII-83-2, flown by 2nd Lieutenant Heighnes Pérez Albela, arrived at Puerto Pizarro at 1505

The Curtiss Cyclone Falcon serial XXXII-82-3 being armed with four 50kg bombs, of Italian origin, before departing for an armed reconnaissance mission from Puerto Pizarro forward seaplane base. (Humberto Currarino Collection)

Tumbes, 31 July 1941: North American NA-50 and Douglas 8A-3Ps being readied by ground crews shortly before the launch of missions on that date. (IEHAP)

hours. This aircraft – part of *83 Escadrille* – arrived to provide fighter escort for *82 Escadrille* seaplanes following MMA directives.

72 EIT – No aerial activity registered.

105 ET – This unit ferried troops to Machala and Santa Rosa, returning to Piura and Chiclayo with war booty.

3 August

XI EB – No aerial activity registered.

XXI EC – No aerial activity registered.

XXXI EIA. – No aerial activity registered.

XXXII EIM – Cyclone Falcon serial XXXII-82-1 took off from Puerto Pizarro at 0100 hours and headed north towards Guayaquil. Taking advantage of the full moon, the pilot, Captain Duarte, and his gunner/observer, 2nd Lieutenant Fernandez, patrolled over the gulf looking for any sign of Ecuadorean Navy vessels. At 0400 hours, 2nd Lieutenant Fernandez saw a convoy heading southbound at an approximate speed of 6 knots. The convoy comprised a tugboat, two ships, two sloops and a large barge.

At 1450 hours, Cyclone Falcon serial XXXII-82-3, flown by 2nd Lieutenant Perez Albela and carrying 2nd Frigate Lieutenant O. Corpancho, departed from Puerto Pizarro and headed north looking for the convoy sighted earlier that morning, discovering it 3km north of the Chaguana River. Besides the six units originally identified, they discovered a double-deck steamer, identifying it as the BAE *Alfaro*. The Falcon crew immediately sent a ballast message about these ships' presence to BAP *Guardian Rios*, which was moored at Puerto Bolívar.

72 EIT – No aerial activity was reported.

105 ET – This unit continued ferrying Peruvian Army troops from Tumbes to Machala and Santa Rosa. In the meantime, the MMA had assigned the Junkers Ju-52, serial OA-HHA *Huascarán*, under the command of the 105 ET to support the unit in its transport duties, speed up the troops' mobilisation to the front and transport war booty to Lima.

4 August

XI EB – No aerial activity registered.

XXI EC – No aerial activity registered.

XXXI EIA – No aerial activity registered.

XXXII EIM – The unit continued with maritime search activities. Captain Duarte and 2nd Lieutenant Davila departed Puerto Pizarro aboard Cyclone Falcon, serial XXXII-82-3, heading for Guayaquil to perform a reconnaissance over the gulf, looking for Ecuadorean Navy activity. Additionally, they flew over the El Faro zone, looking for artillery positions, but without success. Upon its return, the crew reported the presence of Ecuadorean Navy units anchored in Guayaquil port and a convoy north of Punta Piedras.

72 EIT – No aerial activity registered.

105 ET – The formation continued ferrying troops and war matériel back and forth between Tumbes, Machala and Santa Rosa.

5 August

XI EB – On operational alert.

XXI EC – On operational alert.

XXXI EIA – Two reconnaissance sorties were flown by the *91 Escadrille* over the Pasaje-El Guabo-Dos Bocas-Bajo Alto and Puente

An interesting and unique image that shows in detail two important details of the Ca.310 Tipo Perú: the Lanciani-Alfa 2 turret and one of the four vertical containers for anti-personnel bombs or *Spezzionere*. (Sergio de la Puente Collection)

Tumbes forward airfield, 31 July 1941: aircraft from the XXXI EIA awaiting the start of operations. (Amaru Tincopa Gallegos Collection)

Ground personnel seen getting their hands dirty on the maintenance of the Wright R-1820G engine of this 8A-3P, while the sidecar used as transport by the official TON photographer waits patiently. Note the sidecar driver wears an Italian M33 helmet. (Amaru Tincopa Gallegos Collection)

Lieutenant Rafael León de La Fuente (centre) and his crew, Sub-Officers Sanguinetti and Tasso, next to their Caproni Ca.310 bomber at Tumbes on 10 August 1941. Note the insignia of the XI EB. (Humberto Currarino Collection)

Uzcurrumi-San Sebastian-Girón axis. *92 Escadrille* also made two sorties and performed reconnaissance missions over the Aragoto-Macará-Loja-Conzamana axis.

XXXII EIM – Patrolled the Guayaquil gulf in the morning and afternoon, looking for Ecuadorean Navy activities.

72 EIT – Following directives contained in Mission Order No.30, Lieutenant García Romero departed Tumbes to reconnoitre over the

Arenillas-Piedras-Puente Moromoro axis, following the railroad that linked these villages. Aboard his Fairey Fox serial 72-3 was 2nd Lieutenant Pinillos as observer. Additionally, they reconnoitred the Quebrada de Lajas and Puerto Puyango sector, verifying Ecuadorean Army activity in these locations.

105 ET – The unit had one of its aircraft undergoing maintenance at Piura, while another continued to transport troops and equipment between Tumbes and the occupied territories.

6 August

XI EB – No aerial activity registered.

XXI EC – No aerial activity registered.

XXXI EIA – The *91 Escadrille* launched a reconnaissance sortie over Machala.

XXXII EIM – 2nd Lieutenant Pérez Albela departed at 1620 hours aboard Vought 83-2 and, following the El Oro province coastline, discovered a number of vessels – of different size – heading north carrying civil and military personnel in what looked like an evacuation of the province. Additionally, Perez Albela delivered a message to BAP *Almirante Guisse*, containing a sketch showing the Ecuadorean ships' position.

72 EI. – From 5 August to 30 September, Lieutenants Carlos Márquez and García Romero, accompanied by 2nd Lieutenants Hernan Muñiz, Francisco Cavero and Dante Monge, performed daily observation and reconnaissance sorties over the villages of Pasaje, Guabo, Tendales, Costa Rica, San Francisco and the Jubones River mouth.

105 ET – Caproni 105-3 transported a group of TON officers from Tumbes to Machala.

7 August

XI EB – No aerial activity registered.

XXI EC – No aerial activity registered.

XXXI EIA – *91 Escadrille* launched a reconnaissance sortie over Machala and the surrounding area.

XXXII EIM – No aerial activity registered.

LI EA (LI *Escuadrón de Aviación*) – At 0500 hours, Lieutenant Morzán took off from Cabo Pantoja EP garrison aboard TravelAir B-6000S, serial 101-4, heading north-west to perform a reconnaissance over the nearby Ecuadorean garrison of Rocafuerte, located on the Napo River. After overflying the area several times in order to observe the size and characteristics of the forces quartered there, Lieutenant Morzán returned to base and issued a report.

72 EIT – No aerial activity reported.

105 ET – Caproni Ca.111 transports serials 105-4 and 105-5 began to ferry injured soldiers between Santa Rosa and Tumbes.

8 August

General maintenance was carried out for all aerial units. Ground crews from the different squadrons were kept busy working during the day in order to maintain the operative level of their respective units. No air activity was scheduled.

9 August

XI EB – No aerial activity registered.

XXI EC – No aerial activity registered.

Vought V-80P serial XXXII-83-2 and Cyclone Falcon serial XXXII-82-3 undergoing maintenance on the beach of Puerto Pizarro, their assigned forward base. (Amaru Tincopa Gallegos Collection)

XXXI EIA – In compliance with Mission Order No.10, an aircraft of the *92 Escadrille* was sent on a mission to capture images of the villages, airports, railroads and highways of the territories controlled by Peruvian forces.

XXXII EIM – No aerial activity registered.

LI EA – On operational alert.

72 EIT – No aerial activity reported.

105 ET – This formation began to ferry back to Peruvian territory CAP staff and war booty aboard Caproni Ca.111 serials 105-2 and 105-3.

10 August

XI EB – No aerial activity reported.

XXI EC – No aerial activity reported.

XXXI EIA – The *93 Escadrille* flew to Sullana airfield at the request of the EP 8th Light Division commander.

XXXII EIM – No aerial activity reported.

LI EA – On operational alert.

72 EIT – On operational alert.

105 ET – Two aircraft continued to ferry troops and war equipment from Machala and Santa Rosa to Tumbes.

11 August

XI EB – On operational alert.

XXI EC – On operational alert.

XXXI EIA – Both the *91* and *92 Escadrilles* launched reconnaissance sorties over occupied territory.

XXXII EIM – On operational alert.

LI EA – During the morning, the unit sent two Cyclone Falcons and a single Travelair in support of the EP offensive launched against the garrison at Nuevo Rocafuerte (which was captured later that day). Shortly after, Lieutenant Morzan took off aboard the Travelair B-6000S on a reconnaissance sortie over the Napo and Aguarico Rivers, which were both used as escape routes by the withdrawing Ecuadorean forces, discovering their shelters in the process. With the precise location of the withdrawing Ecuadoreans found, the head of the 5th Division ordered the *81 Escadrille* to dispatch a pair of Cyclone Falcons, each armed with four 15kg bombs, to harass the retreating forces. Captain Balarín and Lieutenant Benavides flew this mission, which was completed without incident.

2nd Lieutenant Rolando Gervasi poses in front of one of the Ca.114s assigned to *43 Escadrille* at Sullana in August 1941. (Amaru Tincopa Gallegos Collection)

One of the two Curtiss BT-32 Condors assigned to the 105 ET at San Ramón airfield in August 1941. These, together with a third aircraft assigned to the *29 Escuadrón Commando*, were the only survivors of the four BT-32s that arrived in Peru in 1935. (Amaru Tincopa Gallegos Collection)

72 EIT – No aerial activity registered.

105 ET – The unit continued to ferry both personnel and captured equipment from El Oro province to Tumbes.

12 August

Ground staff from the different units assigned under the 1 GA command spent the day providing repairs and maintenance to their aircraft.

LI EA – Two Curtiss aircraft from *81 Escadrille* took off from Itaya

Civilian and military personnel in front of one of the 8A-3Ps from the XXXI EIA at Talara during a pause in operations. (Amaru Tincopa Gallegos Collection)

A nice view of a silver doped Stinson-Faucett F.19 transport and passenger monoplane during a supply mission to the western Amazon on behalf of the TONO. Silver dope was a process in widespread use around the world in the 1930s which made the skin of an aircraft smooth, increasing speed by up to 30kmph. (Amaru Tincopa Gallegos Collection)

Hacienda Uchugay villages, and the second over the Pasaje-El Guabo-Bajoalto axis.

XXXII EIM – No aerial activity registered.

72 EIT – No aerial activity registered.

105 ET – No aerial activity registered.

14 August

XI EB – On operational alert.

XXI EC – On operational alert.

XXXI EIA – The *91* and *93 Escadrilles* launched a reconnaissance over the Zapotillo-El Huásimo and La Ceiba-Saucillo-Célica areas, at the request of TON command.

XXXII EIM – On operational alert.

LI EA – The *81 Escadrille* launched four armed patrol sorties during the day, strafing and bombing the Ecuadorean garrison at Lagartococha, as well as vigilance posts over the Aguarico, Yasuni and Arcadia Rivers. In its last mission, the *escadrille* met up with the river gunboat BAP *Amazonas*, which provided the aircraft with fuel and ammunition. Shortly after, the *81 Escadrille* returned to Iquitos after completing 18 combat sorties in the area.

72 EIT – No aerial activity registered.

105 ET – No aerial activity registered.

23 August

The 5th Division began planning an operation to clear the Pastaza River and its confluence with the Bombonaza area from Ecuadorean infiltration after several Ecuadorean Army raids were reported in these sectors. The division's HQ requested the support of the BAP *Amazonas* and a single Cyclone Falcon from the *81 Escadrille* to accomplish this mission.

seaplane base in Iquitos to attack Ecuadorean forces in Lagartococha and Redondococha, both located on the Ecuadorean side of the border, as well as other objectives discovered along the Aguarico, Arcadia and Yasuni Rivers. Meanwhile, Captain Balarín aboard Travelair B-6000S serial LI-101-4 from *101 Escadrille* flew from Itaya to the garrison at Nuevo Soplin, near Andoas, carrying medicines and ammunition to prepare the defence of the area in the event of an Ecuadorean counter-attack. After four hours navigating in adverse weather, Balarín successfully reached his destination, carrying seven Ecuadorean prisoners back to Iquitos, during his return flight.

13 August

XI EB – On operational alert.

XXI EC – On operational alert.

XXXI EIA – the *91* and *93 Escadrilles* launched two reconnaissance sorties, the first over the villages of Pasaje, Puente Uzcurrumi and

25 August

The operation to expel Ecuadorean forces infiltrated on the Peruvian shore of the Bombonaza and Pastaza Rivers began in the early hours. The Cyclone Falcon LI-81-1, commanded by Captain Balarín, departed at 0530 hours and reached the Sahuin River three-and-a-half hours later, joining ground forces from Soplin that had just left the Huachi garrison. Using the river as an operational base, Captain Balarín performed three armed reconnaissance sorties over the Pastaza-Puesto-Puyas axis.

27 August

During a reconnaissance mission over the Pastaza River aboard Cyclone Falcon serial LI-81-1, the head of the *81 Escadrille*, Commander Manuel Escalante Pérez, discovered an Ecuadorean aircraft overflying the area and promptly started a pursuit. Unfortunately, the lower performance of his biplane forced him to give up the chase, landing shortly after at the Soplín River garrison.[1]

28 August

After completing their preparations, Peruvian forces began the assault against Andoas, which was occupied by dawn. Captain Balarín, aboard the Curtiss serial LI-81-2, landed there at 0800 hours, receiving orders to perform a reconnaissance sortie over the confluence of the Bombonaza and Pastaza Rivers searching for Ecuadorean troops retreating over the border. During this mission, Balarín discovered a group of troops heading north and made to attack them, but promptly aborted when he saw a soldier waving the Peruvian flag. Balarín, concluding that the area was already under Peruvian control, proceeded to return to Soplín. This was the last mission performed by the *81 Escadrille*, thus ending LI EA involvement in the TONO. The next day, Balarín returned his aircraft to Teniente Gustavo Cornejo seaplane base on the Itaya River, near Iquitos.

10 September

XI EB – The 1 AG command ordered the withdrawal of all units stationed in Tumbes to Teniente Coronel Pedro Ruiz Gallo air base at Chiclayo. However, during mobilisation a Caproni Ca.310 Tipo Perú bomber, serial XI-11-1, flown by Captain Roberto Buenaño, suffered an engine failure during take-off, crashing at the end of the runway.[2] The aircraft burst into flames, but its crew was able to escape from the blazing wreck uninjured. Due to the lack of an emergency response team on the airfield, the aircraft burned out and was declared a complete loss.

11 September

After a bloody ambush set by Ecuadorean forces for a Peruvian Army cavalry patrol in the Porotillo area, TON command ordered XXXI EIA and XXXII EIM to launch attacks against Balao, Tenguel and the right bank of the Jubones River against any Ecuadorean Army units discovered in the area.[3]

XXXI EIA – Three Douglas 8A-3Ps from the *92 Escadrille* flew to Porotillo and Uzcurrumi, where they attacked Ecuadorean positions.

XXXII EIM – No aerial activity registered.

One of the several Stinson-Faucett F.19 transport monoplanes acquired by the CAP to provide transport with the *54 Escuadrón de Transporte* and the *LI Escuadrón de Aviación* in the Amazon forest. This particular aircraft is shown in Ancón in September 1941. (Amaru Tincopa Gallegos Collection)

2nd Lieutenants Wensjoe, Maguiña and Ruiz in front of a Caproni Ca.114 fighter from *42 Escadrille* at Tumbes in early October 1941. (Amaru Tincopa Gallegos Collection)

An officer in a more relaxed attitude as the conflict came to an end in early October 1941. (Amaru Tincopa Gallegos Collection)

Tumbes forward airfield in late August 1941, showing a mixed group of aircraft including a Ca.111 transport, a trio of Ca.114 fighters and a single Curtiss model 37F employed as a hack. (IEHAP)

26 September

XXXII EIM – *82 Escadrille* was ordered to perform an armed reconnaissance sortie around Santa Rosa. The unit command ordered 2nd Lieutenant Heighnes Perez Albela and Sub Officer Manuel Polo Jiménez to take off aboard the Cyclone Falcon serial XXXII-82-3 to perform this mission. Although Perez Albela did not belong to the *82 Escadrille*, he was chosen to take part in this mission due to his position as chief of Ancon's photographic section. Sub Officer Polo Jiménez, on the other hand, had vast experience on these missions and had worked previously with him as photographer in the squadron.

After leaving Puerto Pizarro, Perez Albela and his photographer arrived over Santa Rosa after a flight of nearly an hour at approximately 5,000ft. Once over their objective, Perez Albela began positioning his Cyclone Falcon for the photographic passages, spending nearly 25 minutes taking the images required by the mission. As they were returning to Puerto Pizarro, Polo Jiménez requested Perez Albela to alter his flight pattern to allow him to photograph the Jubones River mouth, where he suspected the presence of Ecuadorean troops. The pilot complied with the photographer's request and turned east, and, as they approached the area, were met by a series of explosions from well-camouflaged anti-aircraft batteries below. Shrapnel from one of the shells exploding around the aircraft hit Polo Jiménez on the head and he fell into the cabin floor with a shattered parietal bone. Despite his severe injuries, Polo Jiménez managed to remain conscious during the return flight to the base, using Perez Albela's kepi to cover his injury and keep blood loss to a minimum. After landing, the pilot called ground personnel for urgent help to retrieve the injured aviator from the aircraft.[4]

After this mission, the head of the 1 AG ordered a halt to all operations over the occupied territories and, shortly after, the units remaining in the TON completed their return to their home bases.

Acta de Talara

Facing a delicate political situation at home and abroad, by 31 August 1941 the government of Ecuadorean president Carlos Albert Arroyo del Río decided to redeploy most of the Army to protect Quito. Based on intelligence obtained from Brazil, Chile and the USA – all of which informed del Río that Peruvian forces were less than 48 hours' march from Guayaquil and in the process of already capturing Machala and Puerto Bolívar – an order to this effect was issued with great urgency. Moreover, according to reports from the same sources, Peruvian troops were also less than 170km from the Guayaquil metropolitan area, and the orders of the Peruvian military were – in case Ecuador

continued to neglect Peruvian rights over the provinces of Tumbes, Jaén and Maynas – to assault and capture the main Ecuadorean harbour. With Guayaquil occupied, Peruvian forces in the Ecuadorean *sierra* (mountains) would head north from Loja, less than 600km from the capital, and begin the military occupation of Quito, an operation that, considering Ecuadorean forces had practically ceased to exist by September, would last a maximum of 10 days.

By the end of August 1941, Peruvian forces had taken the regions of Sucumbios, Napo and Pastaza in the areas corresponding to the former Quijos Governorate, which, in accordance with the Royal Decree of 15 July 1802, went to the Viceroyalty of Peru and were taken by Ecuador during the Pacific War of 1879-83 between Peru and Chile.[5] The advance of Peruvian forces, however, stopped at these points and no further territorial claims were made.

However, pressure by the United States, which was eager to keep the peace in its "backyard", forced both countries to accept definitive peace conditions. A preliminary solution was prepared by the observer countries (Argentina, Chile, Brazil and the United States) and, on 2 October 1941, both parties signed the Talara Act in the Peruvian city of the same name. One of the main points of the peace agreement was the establishment of a "demilitarised zone", comprising the Ecuadorean territories occupied by Peruvian forces, instead of the immediate return of these areas. This was seen by Quito as a form of blackmail by Lima to force the Ecuadorean government to accept a future solution on terms favourable to Peru.

The signing of this agreement allowed both governments to gradually normalise their relationships, thus clearing the way for a bilateral reduction of military forces along the border. Accordingly, the Peruvian armed forces high command ordered the gradual return to their respective home bases of all aerial units deployed at forward operating bases, giving their crews a welcome rest as well as allowing much-needed repair and maintenance to their aircraft.

It is commonly accepted by most academics that the operations carried out by te Peruvian forces represented an act of reprisal, recognised in international law, with the objective of forcing Ecuador, *manu militari*, to respect the rights of Peru over its territorial claims, and not one of territorial conquest or dismemberment. This proved to be especially true when Peruvian forces ended the occupation, on 12 February 1942, of the conquered territory after the signature, by Ecuador and Peru, of the Rio de Janeiro Limits, Peace and Friendship Protocol on 29 January that year.

EPILOGUE

The signing of the *Acta de Talara* put an end – at least for a few years – to the border tensions between the two countries and, during the years to follow, both nations completed the demarcation of at least 90 per cent of their shared frontier. Some years later, in 1960, Ecuadorean President José María Velasco Ibarra declared, before taking office, the Rio de Janeiro Protocol null and void. He said the treaty had been signed during the Peruvian military occupation and was thus illegal and contrary to the other Pan American treaties, having been signed under pressure, despite its ratification by the Ecuadorean Congress on 28 February 1942. Velasco Ibarra also declared the treaty to be unenforceable, adducing presumed inconsistencies between the limits established by the protocol and the geographical reality, as well as "to have been signed under the pressure of a foreign force occupying its territory" and, thanks to this, a 78km portion of the border was left unmarked. Over the following decades this was to cause several incidents and two major conflicts between the countries, which finally ended only on 26 October 1998 with the signing of the Brasilia Act. The latter ratified, 56 years after its signing, the validity of the Rio de Janeiro Protocol, closing definitively a chapter that for more than 50 years bled – physically, geographically, economically, morally and humanly – both countries.

Eclipsed by the events then taking place in Europe, Africa and the Pacific, the border conflict of July-October 1941 between Peru and Ecuador marked the consolidation of military aviation as a cornerstone in modern military warfare for both countries. It became clear that, even in a conflict between relatively small forces, aviation

Crews from XI EB formed during a ceremony for the "official" end of operations held in Tumbes on 1 August 1941.

After the conflict, the CAP fighter force became severely diminished in strength with only four NA-50 remaining as first line fighters after the Ca.114 fighters were sent to second-line duties due to obsolescence. The situation improved in September 1942 with the arrival of the first Curtiss Hawk 75A-8 fighters (visible in this photograph), acquired via the military assistance programme signed with the United States. (Amaru Tincopa Gallegos Collection)

The arrival of 20 Curtiss-Wright CW-22B Falcon monoplanes in 1942 allowed the creation of new reconnaissance units in the form of the *15 Escuadrón de Información Terrestre* and the *35 Escuadrón de Información Terrestre*, which replaced the – meanwhile disbanded – 72 EIT. (Amaru Tincopa Gallegos Collection)

A CW-22B from *15 Escuadrón de Información Terrestre* following a crash landing at Capitán Guillermo Concha Iberico air base in Piura, one of several former airfields that were upgraded shortly after the conflict. (Amaru Tincopa Gallegos Collection)

was fundamental for ground forces to dislodge adversaries and, after breaking them, begin a push inside their territory. After denying the use of the sky to the enemy, the CAP managed to perform attack, recognition and transport duties without problems, and therefore provide invaluable for the Peruvian advance, allowing the ground and naval forces to operate unmolested in the prosecution and achievement of their objectives.

BIBLIOGRAPHY

Corodero, S.E., 'Los Gobiernos de la Crisis de 1859-1860', *Edufuturo*, 2 March 2010.

Hagedorn, D., *Latin American Air Wars 1912-1969* (London: Hikoki Publications, 2006).

Idrovo, H., *Fuerza aérea ecuatoriana: historia ilustrada* (Quito: Ed. Ecuador, 1999).

St John, R.B., *The Foreign Policy of Peru* (Boulder, Colorado:, Lynne Rienner Publishers, 1992; ISBN 978-1-55587-304-2).

Murgia, J.J.E. & Nieto Vélez, A.S.J., 'Conflicto Peruano-Ecuatoriano 1858-1859', *Historia maritime del Perú*, Vol.6/4th edition (Lima).

Naranjo, M.G., *Manual de Efemérides: Lecciones de historia del Ecuador* (Tipografia El Vigilante, 2007).

Paredes, S. de & Weston Van Dyke, H., *A study of the question of boundaries between the republics of Peru and Ecuador* (Washington DC: Press of B.S. Adams, 1910).

Sater, W.F., *Chile and the War of the Pacific* (Lincoln, Nebraska: University of Nebraska Press, 1986; ISBN 978-0-8032-4155-8).

Ureta, E., *Apuntes sobre una campana (1941)* (Madrid: Ed. Antorcha, 1953).

Various, *Historia aeronáutica del Perú, Tomo VI* (Lima: Instituto de Estudios Histórico Aerospeciales del Perú, 1984).

Zook, Z.M.H., The Ecuador-Peru Dispute (New York: Bookman Inc. 1964).

NOTES

Chapter 1

1 1810 was the last year of effective Spanish Crown government over its colonies before the Napoleonic invasion.
2 St John, p.58
3 Murguía *et al*, p.492
4 Paredes *et al*, p.255; St John, pp.58-59; Murguía *et al*, pp.493, 496, 500; 'La Marina de Guerra en la República Siglo XIX: El Conflicto con el Ecuador (1857-1860)', *Marina de Guerra del Peru*, 17 September 2009.
5 Corodero.
6 Sater, p.37
7 This treaty was named after Fabio Lozano Torrijos, the Colombian plenipotentiary, and Alberto Salomón, his Peruvian counterpart, who signed the agreement on behalf of their respective governments.

Chapter 2

1 Promulgated on 18 February 1929 during President Augusto B. Leguía's administration.
2 Issued on 12 March 1936.
3 APRA stood for '*Alianza Popular Revolucionaria Americana*' ('American Popular Revolutionary Alliance'), a Peruvian political party initially planned on a continental scale, with a centre-left position and a member of the International Socialist movement.
4 Caproni Peruana Factory personnel modified two of these machines to flying ambulance configuration at Chiclayo. This conversion was the first of its kind – as far as it is known – in Latin America.
5 Two aircraft confiscated by the Peruvian government from the *Deutsche Lufthansa* Peru Branch on 1 April 1941. These were OA-HHC-304, construction number 5272, christened "*Huandoy*", and OA-HHA-294, factory number 5283, christened "*Huascarán*".
6 Designation given to the export version of Northrop A-17 equipped with a 1,000hp nine-cylinder Wright R-1820 engine and air brakes.
7 Originally assigned to the 83 EC, became an *ad hoc* unit member from 6 August 1941.
8 TON's Headquarters had a limited stock of fuel and lubricants, lodging quarters, food and storage services as well as radio communication systems.
9 Connection airfield improved with lodging, food, communication and storage facilities by 5 July 1941.

Chapter 3

1 Survivors of six aircraft purchased in 1936.
2 Purchased in 1934.
3 Survivors of eight aircraft purchased in 1935.
4 Ecuadorean-German Society of Air Transport.
5 Pan American-Grace Airways.
6 These could carry light bombs and were armed with a pair of 0.30 calibre machine guns, one fitted in the landing gear fairing and the other on a flexible position in the rear cockpit.

7 *Historia Ilustrada de la FAE*, October 1999, p.66

Chapter 4

1 Both remaining units were in Chiclayo, at the disposal of the Squadron Command, and the other in Lima, in maintenance tasks.
2 Factory number 50-952.
3 Factory number 4059.
4 According to official reports by their comrades, Quiñones kept control of his aircraft and headed towards the enemy positions, crashing his bomb-loaded aircraft into them. On the other hand, Ecuadorean reports point out that Lieutenant Daniel Estrada hit the Peruvian aircraft with fire from his ZB.30 machine gun, causing it to fall out of control 100 metres away from Ecuadorean positions.
5 Factory Number 370. This aircraft was a support sent from Las Palmas and was a member of the former XIV Bombing Squadron dismantled at the end of 1940.
6 *Espezones* were 1kg and 2 kg cylindrical grenades specially designed for anti-personnel use, launched in trail at low level over troop concentrations.
7 Ecuadorean sources even invented a Japanese last name for the imaginary pilot, and therefore the "Lieutenant Omira" legend persists to this day. It is worth mentioning that such a name does not appear in either the registers of the XXI Fighter Squadron or in the CAP order of battle for 1st Air Group.
8 The terrestrial complement of an air unit comprised the staff required to operate it.
9 The flight complement of an air unit comprised aircraft and their crews.
10 "Chatas" are flat-bottom boats.
11 Argentina, Brazil, Chile and the United States of America.

Chapter 5

1 Most likely a Curtiss-Wright CW-19R operating from Riobamba.
2 Factory number 437.
3 The incident, known as the Porotillo Ambush, was an action that took place on 11 September 1941 between a Peruvian reconnaissance group and Ecuadorean troops (composed of a squad of the "*Yaguachi*" group, of the "*Montúfar*" engineers battalion), concluding with the almost total annihilation of the Peruvian unit.
4 Due to the severity of his wounds, Sub Officer Polo Jiménez unfortunately passed away in Lima on 22 December 1941.
5 The government of Quijos was a territorial, political and military division of the Spanish Empire created in 1559 in what is now eastern Ecuador, mainly the province of Napo. This government took several names, among them the government of the Quijos, province of Los Quijos, Sumaco and La Canela, government of Quijos, Canelos and Macas, etc.

ACKNOWLEDGMENTS

The author wishes to express his gratitude to the following individuals and institutions for their collaboration in the completion of this book: Major FAP José Rolando Barrera, Sergio De la Puente, Eduardo Espinoza Mora, *Instituto de Estudios Históricos Aeroespaciales del Perú* (IEHAP), Dan Hagedorn, *Museo Aeronáutico del Perú* (MUSAR) and Tom Cooper.

ABOUT THE AUTHOR

Born in Lima, Peru, in 1977, Amaru Tincopa Gallegos is a graduate in law. He developed a strong interest in history at a very young age, and began researching and publishing about Peruvian and Latin American military aviation history.

His first book, covering the deployment history of the *Aeroplani Caproni* and that Italian company's endeavours in Peru for an Italian publisher, was released in 2003. Since then he has published a dozen additional titles in Argentina, France, and the United Kingdom, while three others are in preparation. Amaru Tincopa Gallegos is currently cooperating with numerous renowned military aviation history magazines around the world. This is his second instalment for Helion.